SUDDEN ENDINGS

SUDDEN ENDINGS

Wife Rejection in Happy Marriages

Madeline Bennett

▼

William Morrow and Company, Inc.

New York

"Gee, Officer Krupke" from *West Side Story* copyright © 1957 by Leonard Bernstein and Stephen Sondheim. Used by permission of Jalni Music, Inc., publisher; Boosey & Hawkes, Inc., agent.

Library of Congress Cataloging-in-Publication Data

Bennett, Madeline
  Sudden endings / wife rejection in happy marriages / by Madeline Bennett.
    p. cm.
  ISBN 0-688-09428-7
  1. Divorce—United States. 2. Divorced women—United States
—Psychology. I. Title.
HQ832.B46 1991
306.89—dc20   90-23702
                                                CIP

Printed in the United States of America

First Edition

1 2 3 4 5 6 7 8 9 10

BOOK DESIGN BY KINGSLEY PARKER

Contents

CONTENTS

Dedication and Acknowledgments

I confess to experiencing a surge of jealousy every time I read an author's tribute to her husband for standing by with encouragement, advice, and hot chocolate during the gestation and birth of her book. Such an expression of gratitude is exactly what I would have foreseen if I had written a book while living in my previous life in which I believed I was one half of a happily married couple.

Absent an intimate partner to serve as muse or midwife, and present a book on the subject of my intimate partner's sudden departure, it seems only fitting to dedicate this book to the irony that it can't be dedicated to my husband since it would never have been written if he were still living at home.

For me to survive the trauma of abandonment, I had to find out why my husband—or any spouse who claimed to be in love with a mate—would walk out after twenty-five years with no apparent conflict or remorse. Obviously, I was missing a gigantic chunk of information about deception in intimate relationships.

In the tradition of rehabilitating oneself by helping others avoid similar tragedies, this book is a labor of discovering and transmitting information on unconscious defenses that I fervently hope will help others act in time to prevent the chain reaction of wife rejection from breaking up their families.

There are at least fifty people—they know who they are—to whom I'm deeply indebted for reading and rereading drafts of either the journal article or the manuscript for this book. After initial encounters with psychotherapists who answered my questions with a stony silence, I was fortunate in finding therapists of an opposite persuasion, who supported my mission to explain wife rejection to the public and assisted me by reading and criticizing the appropriate chapters.

I am everlastingly grateful to my agent and my editor for their advice and patience with the continuous rewrites and for believing that wife rejection is a story worth telling and an alarm worth sounding.

The other group whose generosity made this labor possible is the women who shared their stories of sudden abandonment. Learning about the wife-rejection syndrome helped some to metabolize experiences that were still raw and undigested. For others it was an act of unusual courage and caring to exhume the pain for the sake of contributing to an investigation that might save and protect other families.

Last but foremost, my thanks to my indispensable friends who listened to my grief and gave me understanding and advice at a time when the bulk of my life was deserting me. Defections are contagious when a husband departs. Only the truest friends stay the course. "Thank you" is far too ordinary an expression to acknowledge help and devotion of the first magnitude.

1

Sudden Departure, Sudden Rage

▼

Most writings about separation and divorce have a heroic message: I am a better, fulfilled person for having overcome this adversity. Let me confess on the spot that this writer is not a valiant survivor. This is the work of a woman who could not shake off the hurt and loss of rejection after twenty-five years and who would not be satisfied until she had made sense out of the chaotic disintegration of her marriage.

I write because I have learned volumes in the last four years about the close relationship called marriage and because I am convinced that if I had been better informed before the crisis, our whole family—my husband and I, our three children, and numerous relatives and friends—would be gathering around the Thanksgiving dinner table this year. Unless my husband recovers from his lethal allergy to me, our family will never eat, talk, argue, or laugh together again.

If readers can bear with my need to preserve our privacy by using a pseudonym, I will explain what I think caused my husband to suddenly call off a long, happy marriage and will suggest some steps that others can take to avert a similar calamity.

Just as this is not the account of a gallant, independent woman who rose to great success on the ashes of her marriage, it is not a diatribe against men or a *mea culpa* of regrets for not working harder to make the marriage last.

What happened to us exposes as totally fraudulent the comforting notion that it takes two partners to bring down a marriage. Our marriage succumbed to the fantasies and delusions that germinated inside my husband's head. If there is a villain, it is the dereliction of those in the mental-health field who have withheld vital information about the unpredictable trajectory of human anger.

Here is my story with only slight changes in detail to protect our privacy.

For the last four years I have had to ask myself whether I had been hallucinating for twenty-five years when I believed I was married to an exceptionally nice, very decent person. (I shall call him Arthur.) My children and friends assure me that it was no hallucination.

Our courtship typified the conventional fifties. After meeting off and on at other people's houses for about three years, Arthur looked at me one evening with a special light in his eyes that beamed straight into my heart and hormones. Within a few weeks I was deliriously in love with a man whom I had previously admired from a distance and who seemed to be intoxicated by the same love potion.

It was a storybook romance that continued as a romantic partnership through many good times and only a few that weren't. This was a man tender enough to be in the avant garde of Lamaze fathers, tough enough to lead a significant business, sensitive enough to appreciate fine arts and humanities, committed enough to work for many charitable causes, and consistent enough to be as honest and fair in commerce as he was at home. As for chauvinisms, he absorbed the message of Gloria Steinem as readily as the call of Martin Luther King.

This was a relationship I rejoiced in for twenty-five years. Yes, there were chinks such as how resistant Arthur was to introspection and to admitting he might be wrong. And how hard it was to moderate his tendency to be competitive and punitive toward our middle child—an ambitious, provocative male.

I also chafed over his aversion to collaboration. Gardening, for example, was a joint enthusiasm, but the arrangement was that he ruled his domain and I cultivated mine. There was never to be one fabulous garden to which we both contributed ideas and energy. In retrospect, I realize that our sharing of so many common interests covered up the degree to which he ordained how we spent our time and resources.

To me these seemed like minor discontents, and Arthur for his part rarely complained about traits of mine that must have been very irritating such as my shyness, timidity, and lack of patience.

Whatever our failings, we seemed to complement one another very well. My impression, and one frequently articulated by Arthur, was of our great good fortune. We shared similar values and tastes, derived immense pleasure from each other's company and from our physical relationship, and loved being parents to our children. His vision of aging always included me, and mine, of course, always included him. Because we were invariably supportive and forgiving of one another, there was never a question of mistreatment.

Then there was a thundering failure. Our business was one of the casualties of the recession in the early 1980s. It was a small manufacturing business that had supported us and several hundred employees quite satisfactorily until it was challenged by competition from lower-priced Japanese imports and by the simultaneous insults of a slump in sales and a surge in interest rates.

Compared to life-threatening illness, business failure should be a minor setback; there are possibilities for restructuring and recovery. But the humiliation is scalding. This is the most public of failures. Even though the business was eventually sold without filing for bankruptcy, there were several years of tense, demanding negotiations when prospects for infusing more money and resuscitation would unfold one day and unravel the next. Still the owner of record, you are no longer running your business but running interference with banks and lawyers and creditors and, most excruciating of all, facing employees who have depended on you for their livelihoods but whose futures you can't guarantee.

You are coming up incessantly against your mistakes and your powerlessness. Past successes are vanquished by present failure. No matter how bad the news, it is imperative that you maintain an appearance of confidence and composure in every negotiation. Add another insult: The father and brother who used to applaud your leadership and accomplishments don't miss an occasion to gloat over your diminished status.

Although Arthur grew tighter and tenser and snapped occasionally at the children, he remained in command of his considerable intelligence despite the loss of face and the decline in our economic security. He improved his appearance, reduced his calories, stayed off cigarettes, increased his jogging, took up cooking as a distraction at home, and warded off my concern about his mental health by insisting that he didn't want to talk about the pressure during the hours he wasn't coping with it. His sense of humor was suspended and an occasional tranquilizer or sleeping pill helped to ease tension or counteract insomnia. (It never occurred to me to wonder how under such duress he could remain so supportive and uncritical of me.)

My implicit assignment was to maintain domestic tranquility and keep his spirits from collapsing. The litany he heard from me was that whatever the financial outcome, *we* would survive, and our family would always anchor us. As for adding to our income, my efforts were only token, but he reassured me that I was needed more at home than to relieve the financial burden.

When I felt Arthur was being harsh with the children, I would urge him to admit that the pressure sometimes got to him. I felt that it would be healthier for all of us if he would be more honest about the strain. (Retrospectively, I realize that such a confession—so easy for me—was out of the question for him. He could never admit to such a weakness.)

If people were classified according to their curiosity about behavior and personality, I would be grouped with the more curious. My general reading and academic studies have always included topics in mental health and psychology. That divorce frequently follows a financial crisis had not escaped my notice, but nothing I had read would have suggested that a marriage like ours, marked by harmony and commitment, could be jeopardized by a business failure.

Ours was the kind of family that celebrated accomplishments but also sheltered losses. Arthur and I worked together to make our home a sanctuary, a place where our children found unconditional

12

love, along with expectations that they would monitor their own conduct. They knew that I could be persuaded to change my mind more easily than Arthur and that we both aimed within our family for a justice, imperfect though it was, that couldn't be reproduced in the world at large.

After two and half years of unrelenting tension, the issues of the business were finally resolved. It was bought by investors who merged it with another company, retaining Arthur's services only as a consultant. Along with relief, I developed and dismissed a foreboding that it might be harder for Arthur to overcome the self-reproach and loss of prestige than the reduction in income. From the standpoint of economics, we could still pay our children's college tuition; from the standpoint of self-esteem, a lifetime of work looked worthless. As before, I voiced my admiration and love for Arthur, but never pressed him to wrestle out loud with the conflicts that seemed apparent to both of us.

Previously satisfied with my homemaker status, I was now self-conscious about having been spared the responsibility for supporting a family. The goals I had set for myself were always achievable. My failures were private ones. Never having had the exposure of running a major enterprise, I would never have the sickening experience of presiding over its collapse.

And more important, I was never expected to hide my feelings. There was always someone in whom I could confide my doubts and fears and weaknesses. In my eyes, men like Arthur were disadvantaged to the degree they denied themselves such outlets.

In my rush to regain normalcy, I paid scant attention to subtle changes in Arthur's behavior toward me. He had grown gradually less attentive during the business crisis, but that was to be expected. I even cooperated by reducing my claims on his time. I did not require reaffirmation of his devotion to me—which had always been so clear and unequivocal—for he had never expressed an iota of doubt about the security of our marriage.

My goal was to persuade him to take a vacation, which would give him time and space to ventilate the feelings that had been unexpressed for two years. But he was anxious to develop a new business venture. I was supportive; it didn't occur to me to express more than mild irritation when he began spending one, then two, evenings a week out with his partners-to-be.

Sympathy with his ordeal dictated patience and understanding, and relief that the worst was over fortified me while I waited for the cloud to lift. What I didn't know was that a hurricane was forming. While I was still living in the relationship that was familiar and wonderful, Arthur was withdrawing into another world and shutting me out. When I observed signs of distancing and ill temper, I timidly proposed that he see a therapist, a suggestion he rebuffed.

Finally, I became alarmed over a few instances when he seemed disconnected from reality. A friend was terminally ill and he seemed unable to grasp the enormity of it. Attributing his withdrawal to depression—to me a likely aftermath of our financial trauma—I again urged him to see a therapist. This time his response was unsettling. He admitted that he was seeing a therapist, but cut off further dialogue.

Two months later, over cocktails that were to have preceded dinner and a concert, his face lit up and he divulged his secret. He was having an affair. (His therapist had been urging him to confess.) Would I mind if we changed our marriage to an arrangement? He would continue to live at home but would be free to spend time with his lover. He seemed elated, as if expecting congratulations, and oblivious when I became nauseated. If you have heard a story like this, you may have guessed that his lover was *not* the kind of gorgeous, brilliant, sophisticated woman who makes me feel inferior. Quite the opposite. Nothing about her background and personality suggested that she would be a more suitable mate.

Adultery is a nightmare never to be totally ruled out. I always thought I would say something brave like: "Well, go find out. I'll be waiting." But Arthur sounded thrilled and, I thought, somewhat crazed.

There was another declaration, even more chilling, although I didn't register it at the time: "I feel like a different person." That seemed strange since his appearance was unchanged; only this "don't-touch-me" bravado was new. I suspect now that something equivalent to a cyclone had swept through the inner processors of thought and feeling that he recognized as himself.

14

Interpreting his behavior as bizarre and related to aftershock, I began phoning friends and relatives who were trained in psychoanalysis. This seemed like the kind of irrational, self-defeating behavior they would understand. It seemed to me that something had splintered inside. (Later I would think of "it" as something that had frozen over.)

The reactions varied from disbelief to recognition to reticence. One of my closest friends told me curtly that I had no business asking about what was wrong with Arthur. (What was she hiding?) Another explained that he was on a high that was covering a panic. (That made sense, but why wouldn't she tell me more?) Another advised me "not to act like his mother" and prescribed treatment for me. (How would that help?) Another predicted that he would be spilling anger. (That seemed plausible because he had been strangely unable to admit how angry he was at himself, at his father and brother for deserting him, and at people who had reneged on their pledges during the negotiations.)

Although he began spending time out of the house, he continued to go to parties and events in my company. He seemed to be getting his commands from a new transmitter and to have tuned me out altogether. Besides trying to find a therapist who could mend what I took to be the break in his personality, I pursued a strategy of regular reminders of how much he cared about me and everything we had done together and of what he would be giving up if he pursued this affair. Whatever anger and insult I was feeling was smothered to allow me to focus every particle of mental and emotional energy on reclaiming him.

That he was not averse to seeing a therapist with me I interpreted as a good sign. In pursuit of my conviction that this was a temporary aberration and that patience and therapy would bring back the original Arthur, I visited several psychoanalysts who were recommended to me. The mystery deepened. I asked them to bring us together for dialogue. (They refused.) To meet with me and our children. (They refused.) What's wrong with him? ("He's very confused.") I asked whether he was having a nervous breakdown. (They nodded.) Was there a danger of suicide? (Another nod.) He's seeing Dr. X. Why won't she talk to me? (There are rules of confidentiality.) Would she tell me if he were suicidal? (Not necessarily.)

Then I learned how swiftly a spouse can nullify the past. About three months into the crisis, by which time it was clear that no words or actions of mine could change his outlook or influence his decisions, Arthur phoned one morning and informed me that he was moving in with his girlfriend.

Looking back, I wince at the memory of my self-confidence. I had invincible faith that Arthur would recover his memory of everything we had cherished for so many years. And I was sure that I could count on his excellent character. Even if he had to pursue this affair, he would never lose his concern for my welfare and for the family that meant so much to him. Character, I knew, was more reliable than sexual attraction.

But that was before I learned about narcissistic rage.

I can't pinpoint the moment when Arthur's mood changed, when the euphoria vanished. Just before he moved out, I suggested having dinner at a favorite restaurant. His hoarse reply was quixotic. "I can't; you're too angry at me." He seemed to be in a trance.

The third month away he reduced the amount of his check and snarled when I complained. His voice on the phone was hard and icy. I didn't admit it at the time, but he sounded as if *hated* me. The voice was that of a stranger, the demeanor that of an enemy.

Two imperatives loomed: to exert myself to the limit to restore our family, and to find an explanation for this horrendous change in Arthur's personality. The attitude of the therapists—that they were justified in quarantining him and rebuffing my plea for information —both infuriated and incited me.

As tight-lipped as psychoanalysts are in the presence of laypersons, they are loquacious in their writings—and there is no fee for eavesdropping in the library. With perseverance and a psychological dictionary, anyone can penetrate the abstruse, technical language and be rewarded with stunning, and sometimes obvious, insights about our behavior. One principle shouted at me through the first three treatises on "self disorders." Children whose parents were unloving and accusatory seldom develop decent opinions of themselves. Obviously, Arthur had not escaped his abused child-hood as unscathed as I had always thought.

A book that is as eloquent as it is brief is *The Drama of the Gifted Child* by the Swiss psychoanalyst Alice Miller, who has undertaken to demystify psychoanalytic knowledge for general readers. She demonstrates how parents use the brute force of disapproval to rob children of their independence, and how easily children's need for love can be misappropriated by parents to gain control over them.

If we grow up in a home environment devoid of love or receive contradictory messages about love and acceptance, a likely outcome is to be plagued forever with doubts about the value of our person and our work. Adults whose parents allowed them to develop freely and fully cannot fathom the distress that befalls children who reach maturity feeling misunderstood, manipulated, and condemned to a lifetime of proving that they are not the unlovable, incompetent persons who haunt their unconscious.

I realized that I had predicated our mutual understanding on the untested assumption that Arthur's inner world was like mine. I never suspected that growing up with a remote, baiting father and selfish, punishing mother would leave a residue of self-hatred that would put introspection off limits. His assertiveness and stability (verging on stubbornness) had seemed like beacons of strength but could have been stratagems to avoid confronting his self-doubts. My impression of this outwardly confident man was that his child-hood hurts had been neutralized long ago, but really he was walk-ing around with untreated wounds, like someone whose solution for crumbling plaster is to hang a beautiful painting on top of it.

To escape the humiliation of his predicament during the business crisis, he must have sealed off his emotional receptors and literally stopped feeling the pain. The numbing was abetted by denial, the defense that enables us to keep unwanted knowledge out of con-scious awareness. Denial can be a useful defense in situations such as serious illness, when it keeps us unaware of the danger. For Arthur, denial formed a temporary insulation against the shame of public exposure, insulation that would dissolve when he had sur-vived the economic upheaval and had time to reflect on his losses and rate his prospects for a comeback.

17

Defeat, which no one takes lightly, is fiendish for someone whose self-worth depends on day-to-day feedback of success. To keep control of his emotions, Arthur had cultivated what psychologists call a "false self." In childhood he must have learned how to appear confident and composed regardless of his inner turmoil.

What happened after the demise of the business was an extreme form of a common reaction—staying calm during a crisis and experiencing the shock afterward. Arthur's defenses were so overstrained that he could no longer support his denial, the pretense that he could master so many insults.

I believe that feelings of shame, guilt, and anger had been accumulating until his reservoir was full. With the overflow he began experiencing terrifying attacks of panic and fear of losing control—as if his internal compass had gone haywire. Among other gyrations, when it was pointing in my direction, it was no longer pointing toward friend or lover but toward an unwanted intruder. When he finally consulted Dr. X, I suspect that he confided less about his intense suffering than about his sudden inspiration that he would feel whole again if he could only jettison his wife.

The tragic irony was that by the time I gained the insights that would have deepened our communication, Arthur was no longer living at home and I was frantically searching for a couples therapist. The analysts my friends were recommending all wanted to treat me individually and simply ignore my plea for an intermediary to help me reconnect with my husband.

My encounters with therapists whose specialty was couples work left me feeling that skills developed for the purpose of mediating conflict were not applicable to situations in which one partner's internal conflict was spilling over onto the mate.

Finally, after a five-month quest, I found Mrs. S, a therapist trained in psychoanalysis and willing to conduct "couples psychotherapy" (on condition that I see her individually twice a week). By then, the possibility for exploration seemed remote because Arthur wasn't interested in changing (but I, of course, wasn't the least bit interested in giving up). His manner was agitated and distant, yet he was not averse to using the sessions as a forum to enumerate grievances that sounded either petty—I was late meeting him at the movies; I had "forced" him to buy a station wagon instead of sedan—or misdirected—I phoned him too frequently at his office. The latter was dumbfounding: He was confusing me with his mother; she was the one who phoned him incessantly.

In a voice filled with self-pity, he condemned our marriage: "We didn't talk." That was a strange reversal. *I* kept the circuits busy with news of my reactions and moods, but *he* definitely had cut back on his communication.

"What didn't we talk about?" I asked. "You never told me how you felt about your father." I couldn't imagine what I hadn't told him about *my* father, who was always generous with his praise and his worldly goods. But I had never confronted Arthur on the contradictions in his interpretation of *his* father's behavior. He had attributed his father's repudiation during the business crisis to "senility" when in truth his father was in full possession of his faculties.

It seemed ludicrous for Arthur to criticize me for withholding my true feelings about *my* father when that was precisely what he was doing in relation to *his* father, but such turnabouts are the sum and substance of projection, a psychological defense with which I had only a passing acquaintance in those days. This was only a foretaste of what developed later when his confusions multiplied. I was to be mistaken for his mother, his father, and anyone else who had ever been disloyal to him.

Arthur's complaints about our marriage contained one fixation, the pervasive, unshakable conviction that he had never gotten his way. He felt martyred: The concessions and compromises that to me had reflected normal give-and-take between two reasonable people to him represented total surrender to a demanding, manipulative wife. I pointed out that only a very boring person would have been the cipher he seemed in retrospect to have wanted. But my logic, insight, and anguish were superfluous, overruled by his irrefutable need to perceive me as the singular person who had thwarted him.

In an attempt to shock his memory, I appeared at one therapy session in a bathing suit, but he was impassive to the humor and the flirtation.

Whenever I asked him to attend a social event with me, he refused on the grounds that he didn't want to mislead me into thinking that he might come home. His reply was sufficiently contorted to suggest to me that he was still in conflict. I think this was partially true, but I was also engaging in my own form of denial and fantasy. Whenever I listened to a Handel choral work, or saw a marvelous film, or watched a thrilling sunset, I felt absolutely certain that Arthur was longing to share this pleasure with me again. I imagined a scene out of the movies in which he would come running home with his emotional memory restored.

But the trend was in the opposite direction—he was growing more distant and more obstinate. None of this made any sense to my orderly mind until I consulted yet another friend, Betsy, who had made a mid-life career change into psychoanalysis. When she heard my description of the demon who spoke to me on the telephone, her face took on a look of awe and horror: "That demon has a name. It's called 'narcissistic rage.' "

I soon learned that this was a term coined by the late Heinz Kohut, an eminent psychoanalyst, to describe anger that implodes when the core of our self-esteem is lacerated: The fury rages inside and cannot be extinguished. A not uncommon defense is to substitute someone else to take the brunt of it. This is the role I was filling for Arthur the Persecutor, and it was a lifesaving one because if such intense anger turns inward, there is risk of suicide. (That put a new light on the "confidentiality" practiced by Arthur's therapist, Dr. X. By erasing me, she imposed a news blackout on the demise of our family. She could then indulge Arthur's compulsion to unleash his anger on a "safer" person—his faceless wife.)

It was an enormous relief to be confirmed at last. It had taken six months to find a therapist who was not mystified by Arthur's behavior and who felt that I was entitled to information on the pestilence that was devouring my family. Furthermore, Betsy held out hope that with treatment he and we could still make a comeback. I started seeing her by myself in addition to my appointments with Mrs. S.

Betsy was the first person to give me useful advice: "He's in a supersensitive state. Don't make him feel guilty, and don't interpret his behavior. He can't tolerate guilt or any hint that you are controlling him. He will feel violated by the slightest suggestion that you know what he is thinking and feeling. Worst of all—I have to be honest with you—he has acquired an 'allergy' to you; he feels endangered by your physical presence."

Why hadn't Mrs. S told me this? I had just made Arthur feel very guilty for being absent at Thanksgiving. The explanation was simple: Mrs. S didn't know. She was the eleventh psychoanalyst I had consulted and probably the only one who did not recognize what I now call the "wife-rejection syndrome." Since I didn't know what was wrong, I was in no position to screen prospective therapists for their skills or diagnostic insights. Precious months had been wasted, first searching for a willing therapist, then cooperating with an incompetent one.

Mrs. S seemed to be catering to Arthur's projections. Before she could do any more harm, I decided to call off her therapy. But I wasn't prepared for the terrifying change in Arthur. When I next saw him, he was personating the demon on the phone: He looked as if he wanted to murder me. After interviewing several unsympathetic therapists, I fled to Betsy and pleaded with her to try her skills on both of us as a couple. Mercifully, she agreed, and Arthur, perhaps frightened by the intensity of his anger, did not put up any resistance.

Betsy said that her image of people like Arthur is that they have an "internal keep-away catapult"—a mechanism on the style of those medieval firing devices—that gets rid of anger, shame, and guilt by hurling a barrage of blame and recriminations at somebody else.

Betsy confided that it was a shock to see the deterioration in Arthur: a once charming, confident man so frayed and belligerent. "It's a lesson for me not to backdate the condition of a patient. When I observe people defending themselves by firing away at everyone in sight, I usually ascribe it to a lifetime pattern."

What if I had called Betsy in the beginning? I believe, but cannot prove, that there might have been an entirely different outcome. Communication would have been established while Arthur was still in the panic-euphoric phase, before his anger became frozen and targeted on me. A therapist with her training and willingness to help families would also have reached out for our children who were confused, furious, and rejecting of both of us.

As it was, each child was suffering alone. I could not gain their confidence. They did not wish to empathize with Arthur's tragedy—always burdened by fears that he could not measure up to the person he pretended to be—or sympathize with mine—being cast in his unconscious as nemesis, symbol, and substance of the people and forces that had ruined him.

From my talks with Betsy, I realized that a therapist trained to work with both individuals and couples might have been able to help someone like Arthur work through his shame-rage reaction in ways other than running away from me and bonding to somebody else.

I asked her whether there was a name for this behavior. She didn't know any but agreed that it is impossible to call attention to a pattern that has no name. Together we coined some terms:

Wife rejection syndrome to identify the psychological pattern of defending against an overload of anger, shame, and guilt by abandoning your wife (or spouse) and casting her as the stand-in to take the blame for your failings.

Bonding crisis to describe the anxiety that triggers a compulsion to break away suddenly from one intimate relationship and to compensate by forming another.

Chernobyl effect for the allergy or aversion to a person's physical presence—as if that person were radioactive. In wife rejection, the person ostracized is, of course, the wife.

Later I added the term **bad object rage** to the lexicon of wife rejection to describe the most baffling and harmful stage, which Betsy had omitted. To mitigate their self-hatred, the husbands delude themselves into believing that their poisonous feelings have been transferred to their wives. This justifies unquenchable anger and continuous punishment of their wives for being carriers of the bad parts of themselves they wish to disown.

While emotionally I was clinging to my hope for reconciliation, my eyes and ears were informing me that my husband was a different person: Arthur the Protector had metamorphosed into

Arthur the Persecutor, an adversary who could not bear to be in my presence, whose every utterance insulted our past and threatened my future.

The total shock and disbelief that I could actually be facing permanent separation and divorce churned memories of the few flash departures I knew of among our friends, who on the whole are exceptions to the national trend toward divorce and multiple marriages. While lifetime, family-centered marriages may be vanishing species, they are definitely not extinct.

Partially out of despair, partially out of curiosity, I began to trace those faintly recalled stories of terminations that always sounded too implausible to believe. I wondered whether the behavior of those husbands had paralleled Arthur's, whether they too had left in the aftermath of stress or trauma and turned cruel and vindictive.

I did not think about it at the time, but I was actually adopting a method of investigation that was consistent with valid research. I asked first through my network of friends and acquaintances, and later more widely, for introductions to wives or husbands who had been abandoned suddenly by a spouse whom they loved (or valued) and trusted. (If there was a preexisting pattern of hostility, cruelty, alcoholism, or poor character, there would be no gauge by which to measure a change in personality after departure.)

The proposition to be investigated was whether a significant percentage of spouses abandoned suddenly by mates whom they had trusted were subsequently subjected to deliberate humiliation and abuse.

If by means of this informal solicitation, I could generate twenty-five cases of sudden departure by formerly reliable spouses in which abandonment was the kickoff for a prolonged campaign of accusations and harassment, I knew this would indicate that the phenomenon is widespread, at least in the milieu in which I live—middle-class achievers who take life, work, and relationships seriously. (One friend had already noticed that every divorce in her circle had been triggered by the husband's "out-of-the blue" departure.)

I relied on the answers to three categories of questions to separate out the cases of abandonment I wished to study: those that could not have been predicted on the basis of past behavior. I asked the wife for her evaluation of her husband's integrity before his departure, about her expectations for marital longevity, and about the magnitude of shock she experienced at being abandoned. Thus, relationships that had seemed stormy or fragile for a long time were excluded, as were those in which dishonesty or abuse would not have come as a surprise. This line of questioning also screened out marriages that had fallen prey to what is perhaps the most common cause of breakdown, one partner's addiction to alcohol or drugs.

Arbitrarily, I set the time period for a "long" marriage at a minimum of ten years, although in many ways a long marriage can be said to be a state of mind in which the partners have made each other feel secure that their marriage is intended to last.

The symmetry that emerged from in-depth interviews with the first twenty-five women who fit the profile was compelling. All of their husbands had been well regarded in their communities: good citizens and good fathers—middle-class role models. "Out of the blue," and often in a state of euphoria, they exited, deadly serious about grievances that sounded either trivial ("We didn't entertain enough") or fraudulent ("I must do this for self-fulfillment") or distorted ("You overpowered me") or exaggerated ("I was miserable every day of our marriage").

Not one of these men left gently or with remorse. This 100 percent correlation between hasty exits and post-exodus persecution could not be explained by accident. Whatever prompted these husbands to leave so fast must have been linked in some way with whatever prompted them to lay siege to their wives.

After a brief absence, marked by euphoria and comparatively minor aggression, a few of the husbands changed course and applied for passports to return home. Some of the wives cooperated. Others refused, doubting the sincerity of anyone who could seem so uncomprehending about such an emotionally scorching episode.

The elation of the others was as short-lived as Arthur's. Persecution followed. Said one wife, "I still can't believe that my husband, the person I loved best in the world, targeted me for

24

destruction." Said another, "It was as if my husband had declared war on me."

A third wife supplied the caption for before-and-after cartoon frames: "First, he knocked me off my pedestal; then he fed me to the sharks."

2

From Protectors to Persecutors

"I'm afraid I will die if I stay with you."

▼

This chapter is dedicated to Angela, my friend from childhood. It is my apology for never quite believing that Mark, who had always impressed me as a gentle, conscientious, law-abiding, and honorable man, could have repudiated her as violently as she reported. When I found myself in this very nightmare, I had some backtracking to do.

It wasn't that I thought Angela was lying. It was just that my mind balked at believing the facts as she related them. Mark, the big-city doctor who cared enough to make house calls, could not have told her how lucky he felt to be married to her just before he consulted a lawyer about a divorce. There had to have been some warning. He wouldn't just walk out the door two days after she came home from the hospital to recover from a hysterectomy. She must have been exaggerating when she described his malevolence.

In truth, these facts were too painful to absorb, and Angela lived far enough away to free me from an obligation to sort out the contradictory impressions. Although I never became her day-to-day confidante, we continued to include her in our social life. Mark's misdeeds took on a comic dimension in her narration. She learned quickly what I was slow to grasp, that friends squirm away from knowledge that gives them too much discomfort.

The mystery of Mark had always bedeviled me. Why would someone who appeared to admire and value his wife all of a sudden scrap everything, not only his mate but all of the blessings of a long marriage—adoring children, a home brimming with mementos and personal treasures, status in the community, a circle of friends, a family history?

Even now, after accumulating evidence of more than twenty-five husbands repeating the same pattern, I find it almost impossible to square such reckless departures with my model of human behavior.

As the common elements emerge in all of these stories—mine, Angela's, and those of other wives who agreed to be interviewed—it may strike you that the perspective is one-sided, depicting the wives as unrealistically innocent. Though your skepticism is justified, I ask you to withhold judgment until I have developed the psychological evidence to discredit the commonsense notion that "it always takes two to tango" even though one spouse calls off the marriage.

For the moment, let me propose that you trust my characterization based on the logic of eliminating other possibilities. Assume the opposite. Assume that my impression of myself and of the other wives who shared their marital catastrophes is totally a deception. Assume that on the surface we appear agreeable but are really shrews at the core. Would such a supposition be sufficient to account for the double insult of flight and fury? If the husbands truly felt mistreated, why didn't they separate and sue for divorce in a civilized, sequential manner? Why did these men, who had been neither scoundrels nor weaklings by testimony of their wives, inflict such a reign of terror after they absconded?

Here is a sampling of the scenes in which the husbands announced their bonding crises, their urgent need to disconnect from their wives and, in most instances, bond to somebody else. Bear in mind these were all long marriages (ten years was the shortest) that felt stable and satisfying to the wives.

▼

Sean and Cynthia, both of whom were architects, were attending a concert by their local orchestra. In the lobby during intermission Sean cleared his throat, turned to his wife, and announced. "I'm leaving. I'm going home right now to pack my things." He did just that: drove home with Cynthia, stuffed some clothes into a suitcase, scooped up Charcoal, who slept on his side of the bed (leaving behind Fido, who slept on Cynthia's side), and sped away into the night.

▼

Felicia was in her ninth month and moving laboriously around the kitchen fixing dinner when Oliver, a public-relations executive, collapsed on the floor and told her with tears streaming down his face, "I have to leave you because I am in love with another woman."

▼

Harold, a very successful businessman, turned over in bed one morning and said in a matter-of-fact voice, "Fran, I'm leaving you."

▼

Diane and Nick were splurging on an intimate, expensive dinner. Over dessert Nick said he had something to tell her: "I'm in love. I'm having an affair—with a *man*." Diane was thunderstruck. "I never had an inkling during the twenty plus years of our supposedly happy marriage that Nick had any attraction to men."

▼

Kathy rushed into the living room to welcome Alex back from a business trip and found him standing in the doorway. While she hugged him, he kept his arms pinned to his sides. "Standing there like a statue, he told me that he was having an affair with his young assistant and was going to leave me and have a baby with her. Then he reached into his pocket and handed me a consolation prize, an airline ticket to visit my mother."

▼

It was just before the Christmas holidays when Peter, a prominent labor arbitrator, stood before the newly decorated tree and told Priscilla his news. "His voice was filled with excitement when he announced that he was leaving me after eighteen years because he was deliriously in love with his secretary."

▼

Alice was flabbergasted to see Barry—a factory foreman and loving husband and father until the plant closed and he lost his job—pull up to their house in a brand-new sports car, an expenditure that would plunge them further into debt. "Before I could complain, he dropped another bombshell. He told me he had just rented an apartment with a girlfriend."

▼

Lionel, chief of radiology at a leading hospital, was returning with Eleanor from their country house when he blurted out his secret: He had fallen in love with a woman whom he had just met at a weekend retreat for hospital executives.

▼

Natalie returned with her children from a weekend visit to her parents to find that Simon had moved all of his things out of their apartment.

▼

Larry, an economist, felt insulted to the point of leaving government service when he wasn't named to succeed his boss as head of the agency. With Marie's full approval, he had taken a job out of town. "It would have been foolhardy for me to leave my job until we were certain that his new position was working out. The interim arrangement involved his coming home late on Friday and departing Monday at the crack of drawn. One Monday morning there was a note on the dresser saying he wanted a divorce—after nineteen years."

Even as I recount these scenes, I catch my breath at each shocking announcement, just as I did on first hearing. Separation was an accomplished fact. Not one of these husbands said: I am having this awful conflict. I feel as if I have to separate from you, or I think I am falling in love, or I feel terrible about what this will do to you and the children.

And so many wives described their husbands as *elated*. This wonderful thing is happening to me . . . I never felt this way before. . . . I'm getting older and have to fulfill myself right now. . . . I've always been manipulated; at long last I am in charge of my life.

No guilt, only blatant hedonism. I'm doing what feels good to me. This is bliss, and you are an albatross.

No wonder the wives were scared and furious and in no frame of mind to speculate on whether such euphoria or indifference was a symptom of anxiety or panic or a nervous breakdown.

I must repeat that these announcements issued from men who were previously valued by their wives as caring husbands, loving fathers, and citizens well regarded by their peers. It was characteristic that public opinion made not a particle of difference once they decided to leave home. That family and friends were not so jubilant about this form of liberation did not deter them in the slightest. They were flying on automatic pilot.

A word on the patterns of adultery. Co-workers, secretaries, and assistants were named most frequently. Most galling for the wives were the liaisons with their "best friend"—a double betrayal. The impression was of choices governed more by convenience than allure, but the wives would be the first to admit that their opinions might have been biased.

One pattern common to all of the stories is a context of stress, trauma, or crisis. Almost without exception, the wives were extending themselves to help their husbands cope with specific stress, most often related to career setbacks, but death, illness, and aging were other common pressures. Even the worst of these traumas, the death of a child, would have been a cause for suffering but not a threat to a stable marriage.

I think most of the women would have seconded Kathy's perspective: "I could imagine a marriage winding down, but it was inconceivable to me that either my husband or anyone else who had so much at stake in his marriage and family would just walk out the door."

What was invisible, of course, was the increasing tension and the spillover of anger, guilt, and shame that preceded the explosive moment of going public with the bonding crisis. The words were disconcertingly similar. A hot and agitated news flash—"I'm in love with somebody else"—or the cold and final rejection—"I'm leaving *you*. One says, I have a new love so I'm severing my connection to you; the other says only the obvious; I no longer feel connected to you.

Of the first twenty-five women who shared their stories, only Natalie and Cynthia were consciously struggling with marital drift.

▼

Natalie and Simon were having many disagreements. Discord had followed on the heels of Simon's being denied tenure by the sociology department, but Natalie's patience had not run out on her high-school sweetheart. She hoped that they would work together to get his career and their marriage back on track. That was until she came home to find the apartment emptied of his possessions.

▼

With his career in a slide, Sean had become especially envious of Cynthia's success and the fact that she had won a commission to design a housing project for the elderly about the same time that he had been forced to close his architectural office.

"I was confident that Sean would soon be hired by one of the larger firms, since business was finally picking up, and I guess that's why I was so patient with him despite the overt hostility. He had me constantly on the defensive, accusing me of being angry and mean. Afterward, my friends confided that they had been alarmed at being bystanders to his verbal attacks. I guess I was keyed to hold things together, expecting a return to normalcy as soon as he landed another job. When I developed an ulcer, it didn't even occur to me to blame it on his grinding hostility."

*   *   *

Business and professional reverses, similar to those suffered by Cynthia's husband and mine, proved to be among the most common precursors of wife rejection.

▼

Oliver lost face when his public-relations and fund-raising campaigns were not sufficient to save the theater company. Felicia felt this shame was misplaced because the string of artistic failures was not really a reflection on him.

▼

Nick, Alex, and Larry were passed over for the promotions they had counted on.

▼

Barry couldn't shake the shame of joblessness even though he obviously had nothing to do with the closing of the plant. He developed several serious medical ailments including diabetes, but his doctor was even more alarmed by his mental condition. It was obvious to Alice and to his doctor that Barry was rambling and not very coherent. They wanted him to see a psychiatrist, advice he adamantly refused to follow. Some months later their younger son was in an automobile accident in which he sustained third-degree burns to his back and chest. Barry was unable to help: He stayed home and watched television while Alice, who fortunately was a practical nurse, stood vigil in the hospital.

▼

While Lionel's career was flourishing, his relationship with his teenage children was a shambles. Disagreements and disapproval were eroding his earlier rapport with them. Also unsettling was the recent death of his father, leaving unresolved their lifelong conflict.

Death of the father was cited by several wives as a demarcating event.

▼

Priscilla felt that Peter was more disturbed by his father's death than he would ever admit. Accomplished as he was, Peter could never fulfill his father's demanding expectations; his death seemed to liberate Peter to rebel against his stern oversight. According to Priscilla, his father would have condemned Peter for his infidelity and would have thoroughly disapproved of the background of his mistress.

Death and suicide were mentioned frequently as recurring preoccupations.

▼

The most tragic loss had been suffered by Alex and Kathy. Their brilliant son had been killed three years earlier in a boating accident. Part of Alex's "self-discovery" was the prospect of fathering another child with his young assistant. When he handed Kathy the airline ticket, he seemed to be waving a wand so she would vanish and not be a drag on his blooming romance. "This was a one-hundred-and-eighty-degree change from the Alex I knew, who was a dependable workaholic and who fully appreciated my ability to combine work in the business with management of our homelife."

▼

While Mark's departure came as a bolt out of the blue to Angela, the worries she had been harboring pertained to his mental health, not their marriage.

"A few months before I learned that I would have to undergo the hysterectomy, Mark had complained of feeling depressed. He saw a psychiatrist for medication but not for therapy. His depression was particularly ominous because it coincided with reaching the age at which his father had committed suicide. Then my impending hysterectomy seemed to make matters worse. It was mystifying to me that a man in his forties who was already the father of teenage sons should have been so troubled by the loss of his wife's fertility."

After his hasty departure, Mark returned to collect some clothes.

Angela threw the dirty laundry at him, a mild reprisal considering the provocation. "Later he said that he had dreamed that I was pointing a gun at him. That made no sense. He was imagining me wanting to kill him; yet I hadn't 'attacked' him with anything more menacing than a few limp shirts."

▼

Before Nick left for his male lover, Diane had never dwelt on the pattern of suicides in his family as a reason to worry about his mental health. "Nick was the stable one; he was always calming me down."

After his declaration of change in sexual orientation, she feared further shakeups. "He seemed to be operating on half a cylinder. I wanted to know whether the analyst he was seeing was aware of the number of suicides in the family history, but I knew she would only rebuke me if I phoned. She had instructed me never to call again."

▼

Felicia knew that there were times when Oliver was suicidal and that his therapist (who also wouldn't return calls) somehow managed to quiet his anxiety.

▼

When I pressed my husband, Arthur, to tell me whether he was having any thoughts about suicide, he admitted that suicide had crossed his mind a few months earlier. Since he had shown no signs of depression, I surmised that he was surviving the loss of the business about as well as could be expected. After his admission, I naturally worried about whether he was being honest when he spoke of suicidal feelings in the past tense.

Two of the husbands were more specific about their inner distress, having lingered after announcing their bonding crisis, still under the same roof but estranged and sleeping separately. When their wives pleaded with them to remain at home and try to work things out, their answers were as baffling as Arthur's when he refused to have dinner with me because I was "seething with anger."

The words they spoke were virtually identical: "I feel as if I will die if I stay with you." While this may have been a heartfelt response to the nameless terror they were experiencing, the wives can't be blamed for hearing only the rejection.

As word spread about my work on abandonment, more women volunteered accounts of sudden endings to marriages they had judged to be stable and monogamous. The stories were consistent: an outside trauma, similar to the ones described above, but no evidence to link the trauma with the sudden departure. (Only someone knowledgeable about unconscious defenses could make the connection.)

It was hard to account for the haste. Why the lightning departures? Was it the magnetic attraction of the new lover or was there something repelling about the wife? Whether the propulsion was ecstasy or anger, the impression was of an irresistible need to get away as fast as possible. One wife recalled, "You would have thought that a posse were chasing him." Another, "He acted as if I were carrying the plague."

The more I looked into rejection, the more I focused on the incongruity of running away from your wife as if someone had hollered fire and then sending only messages that insult and deprive. My therapist, Betsy, spoke of an allergy. Several wives thought their husbands had developed a phobia. All agreed that "Chernobyl effect" captured the salient behavior—the rejecting husbands acting as if their wives were radioactive.

Not only did the abandoning husbands make no effort to minimize the damage to the family's infrastructure, they seemed to work overtime at intensifying the misery. This is the self-perpetuating anger of "bad-object rage," which psychologists would classify as "ego-syntonic" because the anger is actually fortifying. In their disordered state of mind, they feel *good* about directing a constant stream of recrimination and punishment at their wives.

▼

Lisa's account of sudden rejection left an indelible image of a husband whose vendetta against his wife was totally out of control. A highly educated, upper-income couple (Norton was a successful accountant and Lisa was on the verge of earning her doctorate in art history from a leading university), they were in Lisa's eyes very "happily married." Returning to their apartment from a weekend visit with a terminally ill relative, they found that their contractor had made a botch of installing their kitchen cabinets.

Lisa was very annoyed and told Norton that he would have to help supervise the contractor because the renovation of their apartment was consuming too much of her time. Norton reacted to her demand not just with anger but with demonic fury.

Within seconds Lisa was a battered wife. Her husband struck her across the face, threw her to the floor, grabbed her throat, and bellowed that she was insane and had to be committed to a mental hospital. The next day he actually forced her to accompany him to court where he applied for an order for involuntary hospitalization. Fortunately, a social worker recognized his behavior as abnormal and refused to process his complaint. She advised Lisa to consult either a lawyer or a therapist. Lisa chose to see a therapist.

This sounds like a sudden and horrifying attack of paranoid delusions, which it surely was, but the accusation also showed the specific markings of the transfer of persecutory feelings that go with wife rejection. Norton must have been *in extremis*. We don't have to know much about projection to suspect that he was probably accusing his wife of precisely what he feared was happening to him.

As Arthur was sure I was "seething with anger," Norton was convinced that Lisa was going insane. What they had in common was a desperate need to locate the caldron of boiling feelings in their wives.

One effect of institutionalizing his wife would have been to put distance between himself and the infectious part of him she had come to represent. Failing that, Norton moved out of their bedroom into the spare room.

Norton also formed a new attachment, but not to a lover. He immersed himself in an Eastern religion and talked of an "awakening" and of "fulfillment," in words that seemed to echo the salvation through sexual gratification theme that mystified so many of the wives in the study. His machinations to foist hospitalization and psychiatric treatment on Lisa acquired a religious fervor. "He saw it as his religious duty to take care of me.

"Many months later, a neighbor told me that Norton had phoned about the time of the court incident sounding very disturbed—sobbing and somewhat hysterical. The man was at a loss as to what was wrong or what to do other than give Norton the name of a psychiatrist."

After a second episode of physical violence, Lisa joined a battered women's group but found that her experience was different from that of other members. They told of their husbands' beating them and then being remorseful. A "honeymoon" period would ensue until the violence erupted again.

"There was no 'honeymoon' with Norton. He never said he was sorry. The verbal assaults never stopped. From the moment of that first attack, I was an object of contempt, hatred, and scorn, all cloaked in that bizarre language: 'You're mentally ill, and I'm going to help you.' "

This perpetual state of anger and blaming and being out of touch with regret or guilt is the true and terrible nature of bad-object rage.

Norton's explicit delusion that his wife was having his mental breakdown pervaded their homelife for over two years. "It unnerved me so much that I sometimes thought I *was* crazy. I couldn't concentrate on my writing or teaching and would burst into tears from frustration and fatigue. Over and over I checked my impressions with my therapist; she kept reassuring me that I was not insane."

The first time I spoke with Lisa, she was clinging to the hope that the original Norton would reappear. "We have so much in common: our interests and our backgrounds. Norton was always so stable and reasonable; I was the one given to emotional outbursts."

Learning about wife rejection proved liberating. "I don't feel so trapped by his delusions now that I understand them. He has had me continuously on the defensive. Now I know that I have to protect myself, with a divorce if necessary."

*   *   *

While none of the other wives told of being physically assaulted, several recounted episodes of fury and near-violence flaring suddenly as if the stick of dynamite were already lit.

▼

Diane was horrified by the Nick she encountered at lunch. "The agenda of the meeting was to discuss children and finances, but I really hoped to rekindle our relationship. I couldn't believe that anyone who seemed so authentically heterosexual would persist in a homosexual relationship."

Her hopes for reconciliation withered when she saw his face. "He had a look of cold fury, like the expression of the faces of Gestapo agents in World War Two movies. There was no emotion in his voice when he told me that he wanted me out of his life. The change in sexual orientation suddenly seemed incidental. My husband looked like somebody who wanted to *obliterate* me."

▼

When I met Arthur for lunch about two months after he had left home, I reached up to give him a token kiss, but he dodged, and my lips bumped the back of his head. A few weeks later, at a large reception, he literally shoved me away when I came within kissing distance. There was more than anger in his expression but I couldn't name the other emotions. After I learned from Betsy about his "allergy" and began to grasp that behind the allergy, or Chernobyl effect, was an unconscious terror of being contaminated by me, I realized that the look in his eyes was of *fear*. My beloved husband was actually afraid of me!

▼

It was a physical assault on an adult child that notified Marjory that her husband was no longer the man she had admired and adored for twenty-eight years. Daniel was in his daughter's college town on business. The morning after a pleasant dinner, he charged into her apartment at six A.M. and, to no one's surprise, found her in bed with her boyfriend. Daniel flew into a rage and punched both of them. Daughter and boyfriend tried to calm him during a ride to the airport, but he persisted in shouting and shoving throughout the tense trip.

Nothing about this skirmish meshed with the family's picture of Daniel. They knew him to be "kind, witty, strong-willed, intelligent, and very talented." Ever since returning from a grueling photojournalism assignment covering famine in North Africa, however, he had been brooding and withdrawn. Marjory thought his world had darkened. "He seemed to be living and reliving the suffering of those starving children. They broke his heart. I also think the experience reawakened memories of being overpowered by his cold, disapproving mother."

▼

Daniel's fisticuffs had a verbal parallel in our family.

Arthur and I had gone backstage to congratulate our younger daughter on her performance in a high-school play. Still tense and self-conscious about having missed one of her lines, she criticized Arthur for arriving late. To my mortification, Arthur skipped the praise and began haranguing her for being "inconsiderate"—his voice loud enough to be overheard by the entire cast and backstage crew. This was another incident I wrote off to business stress, but now I think it should have warned me that something much worse than short temper was afflicting Arthur.

▼

If the intensity of Norton's "insanity" rejection was at the severe end of the spectrum, Lionel's brief affair with the hospital executive he had met at the retreat was in the mild range.

It lasted only a few months, and Eleanor endured mainly insults, such as lack of concern for her and contempt for their past—"We have nothing but history together"—but there was none of the recrimination and punishment that characterize bad-object rage.

Of course, there was nothing mild about affairs and insults from Eleanor's perspective. She was relieved by his return but braced for a repetition, no longer confident that their thirty-two-year marriage would last. She did not find their therapist's opinion that Lionel's affair was not really a reflection of his attitude toward their mar-

39

riage very convincing. Only after she learned about the syndrome of wife rejection did she consider the possibility that he had suffered a bonding crisis—an acute need to separate from his wife as a means of coping with a threatened spillover of feelings of guilt, shame, and anger—and that he might be sincere about his renewed commitment to their marriage.

I think that information on the syndrome really helped Eleanor regain trust in her husband. If she had continued to regard his every move with suspicion, Lionel would probably have had another bonding crisis which would have splintered the family.

To find other examples of spouses who were temporarily rejected might be even more daunting than locating permanently rejected spouses. Word-of-mouth might not work as a method of finding spouses to be interviewed who left abruptly and then returned. However, this clear evidence of a range of severity in bonding crises suggests that there must be many Eleanors who swallow the hurt and resume their marriages, but in a guarded manner that almost provokes a repetition.

▼

Priscilla and Peter are an example of a couple who might have survived a bonding crisis if the rejected spouse had had the benefit of information on the syndrome. Only three months had elapsed from the day before Christmas when Peter floated out on his high until the day he floated an insulting proposal for returning home with permission to continue his affair, but during those three months Peter behaved as if he were carrying on a vendetta against his whole family.

When a manila envelope with a slew of bounced checks arrived from the bank, Priscilla was certain that the bank had made an error. However, the self-righteous voice on the phone read out the date on which Peter had closed the account. Not long thereafter, Priscilla had to abort a family trip because her key wouldn't open the car door; the lock had been changed. A couple of weeks later, mother and children were stranded in the corridor outside their apartment at one A.M. While they were away visiting Priscilla's family, Peter had taken advantage of their absence to install a new lock on the apartment door.

It would have been charitable to describe Peter, the labor arbitrator, admired by his family for his intelligence and character, as confused. First, he left home in the heat of passion, having changed his mind about his eighteen-year marriage. Then, he behaved as if he were entitled to repossess his material contributions: the apartment, the car, and the bank account. Did he wonder how his children would interpret those actions? And then his sudden about-face: asking Priscilla to let him move back home without relinquishing his mistress.

This me-first attitude sounds remarkably like the power dreams of a two-year-old. Psychologists call it grandiosity and omnipotence. (I am at the center of the universe I own.) Unlike those of a two-year-old, Peter's ambitions were not curbed by lack of power. Nothing barred him from ordering the bank to cut off the family's funds, from hiring a locksmith to make their doors impassable, and from telling his wife he didn't love her in words that made her feel "like a leftover from a tasteless meal."

The irony about this example of rejection is that Peter stopped being so punitive after a few months. That he was able to contemplate returning home indicated that he was no longer governed by the Chernobyl effect and that their relationship was not to be rocked by the real horror, bad-object rage. The way Peter behaved in the divorce negotiations—as a person who felt responsible for the future welfare of his children and wife of eighteen years—showed that he was in a different frame of mind from the husband who has no compunctions about reducing his family's money supply to zero.

Like Priscilla, I would have found his wife-mistress proposal too degrading to entertain, but would I have felt differently if I had known about the wife-rejection sequence?

Let me pose the question differently. What if Priscilla (or, for that matter, Eleanor) had had a framework for attributing her husband's mischief to wife rejection instead of malevolence. Would she have judged his behavior to be less reprehensible if she were famil-

iar with the syndrome? What if she had known that a hasty, pan-
icky departure was a symptom of a bonding crisis, and that
regression to vindictive behavior unworthy of a two-year-old is to
be expected? Would she have been more inclined to be patient?

With all Priscilla had invested in their long marriage and co-
parenthood, would she have thought it worthwhile to wait and see
whether Peter would recover his original personality and attachment to her? And if wife rejection were well known as a hazard to
family life, wouldn't there be therapists who specialized in helping
families get through these crises? And wouldn't Priscilla have been
on the phone the morning after Peter's announcement, recruiting
such a therapist?

Knowing nothing about the extreme of a bonding crisis—bad-
object rage—Priscilla and Eleanor could take no comfort from being
spared the relentless insults, cruelty, humiliation, and financial
strangulation that are the fate of the wife whose husband continues
to live by and act on the delusion that she is the enemy who ruined
his life.

Before Arthur developed his phobia to me, I never knew him to
be more than momentarily angry. There was really only one occasion during the entire twenty-five years of our marriage when he
seemed intensely angry at me. In retrospect I realize that he was
reacting to an array of slights I was too "logical" to notice.

The incident involved making hotel reservations for the weekend
of our older daughter's college graduation. I decided to economize
by reserving at an inexpensive bed-and-breakfast and mentioned
this to Arthur just as we arrived for a midterm visit—having collected a speeding ticket en route—and just before we discovered
that our daughter had injured her knee badly in a running accident.
Our visit was spoiled by Arthur's reaction to her injury. Instead of
being consoling as I would have expected, he persisted in scolding
her for keeping it a secret, a variation on the backstage scene with
our younger daughter.

On the way home in the car, Arthur suddenly flared up and
excoriated me for making the bed-and-breakfast reservations without consulting him. He must have fulminated for a full five minutes. I suffered the abuse silently, feeling that the issue was too

petty to dwell on and that his temper was inflamed by tension from the business crisis. A few hours later, he apologized, and at graduation, a few months later, he even admitted that I had made the right choice.

Now that I am sensitized to how acutely Arthur experienced wounds to his self-esteem, I realize that a multitude of insults were tucked into that episode. The speeding ticket would have been a minor irritant compared to his chagrin at reacting so unsympathetically to our daughter's injury, contradicting his self-image of being an empathic parent (an image that corresponded to reality until he became so defensive during the business crisis).

My decision about the bed-and-breakfast delivered another insult: It was a reminder of our lowered standard of living. It also breached an unspoken compact, which I had yet to decode, that he was the only one authorized to make hotel reservations.

The last insight about his hegemony over travel plans is the kind that dawns only after you have subjected your entire married life to minute scrutiny. I mention it here because it may unravel some mysteries for a reader.

The more Arthur accused me of controlling, the more aware I became of the power he exerted over me. Travel was an example. I can't remember our having less than a wonderful time on a trip or vacation, but there was always tension over the arrangements. It seemed natural for me to do the research and planning, yet he always sounded dissatisfied with my recommendations. No matter how busy he was, he insisted on making the reservations himself.

As I reviewed my impressions of his childhood, I remembered how he used to joke about his parents' sending him away to camp when he was two and a half so they could go to Europe. (This was before World War II, when transatlantic trips involved week-long ocean voyages.) His parents compounded that desertion by leaving him behind when he was older and primed to see the European capitals that sounded so splendid to him.

No wonder that Arthur forcibly left *me* behind soon after our wedding when I pleaded to go along on a business trip to New Orleans, that he resisted entrusting me with travel arrangements, and that his maneuvers to frustrate travel plans multiplied as the fate of the business was being decided.

On the positive side, it was not surprising that we were in wholehearted agreement about initiating our children into the joys of travel. We laughed and scolded during the years in which their travel adventures seemed to consist mainly of wrestling on the floor of the family station wagon. There was even a cold dip in the icy waters of Jackson Lake after a canoe capsized during a punching match. But as they grew older, their rivalries subsided, and our mutual appreciation of scenery, people, culture, art, and architecture fused us into a family of happy travelers.

My running tally on our family life focused only on the commitment and joy implied in those good times at home and abroad and skipped lightly over the sparring between Arthur and me that somewhat marred the planning phase.

Of course, I overlooked a tense weekend trip to attend a wedding two months before his sudden departure. Arthur actively frustrated every one of my preferences, picking an inconvenient hotel, visiting a relative in whom he had never before expressed interest, and avoiding the special museum show I was primed to see. By the end of the weekend I was so irritated that I accepted a ride back with friends while he returned by plane. Afterward he pleaded ignorance as to why I had found him so uncooperative. I truly think he was so deeply into denial at that point that he was unaware of his hostility. But I, of course, was still blindly confident that his outlook would improve just as soon as we put the trauma of the business crisis behind us.

Having never noticed that travel was an issue that divided us, I was perplexed after his departure when Arthur concocted a grievance regarding my interference with his freedom to travel. He alleged that I had impeded his success by preventing him from making business trips. It was true that I missed him when he was away (as he seemed to miss me), but travel was only a minor aspect of his work and one that was totally beyond my influence.

Each of us has a private catalog of worries, and like mine, they are probably compiled out of memories of the events that saddened the lives of the people close to us. I have always carried around a mega-worry about losing a loved one through illness or accident. I had known enough sudden death and lasting guilt from words of love unspoken to inspire me to keep my family constantly informed about how much I loved and valued each one of them.

For my life (and my children's lives) to be upended by abandonment, a calamity that wasn't even on my worry list, sent me back to reexamine every assumption I had ever formed about relationships.

Every interview added another facet to the accumulating evidence that many wives and husbands are involuntary spectators at the demise of their marriages. It soon become apparent that when a spouse who has never suffered abuse or cruelty runs off with the speed of a purse snatcher, chances are he or she is undergoing a bonding crisis, a form of anxiety that is relieved by severing the bonds to one's mate and forging new bonds to a lover, a religion, someone or something to stave off the panic.

While my interviews were confined to wives, I have no doubt that there is also husband rejection, and that it deserves a book of its own.

If you are not interested in the psychological detective work that brought to light the rejection syndrome, you may want to skip the next two chapters and move on to the accounts of what happened to the rejected wives in the months and years of being miscast as the villains in their husbands' life scenarios.

Believing that the victims of rejection are entitled to an honest portrayal of the hardships, I will not gloss over the cruelty but will also suggest that the grim outcome could be averted if we were better educated about the ways personal stress converts into hostility and distancing toward our spouses. I will suggest that many episodes of rejection could be prevented if the warning signs of rejection were known and if mental-health professionals geared up to help save marriages. I will also argue that the reform in divorce laws known as "no-fault" has proved to be a catastrophe for rejected wives and a windfall for rejecting husbands.

3

I Married You to Reflect My Good Object;
Now I Need You to Stand In for My Bad Object.

▼

It is more than four years now and I am still jolted awake every morning by the shocking knowledge that Arthur, the man I adored, is gone and that someone who looks just like him is my enemy with an agenda dedicated to wiping me out emotionally and materially.

Among the first twenty-five women I interviewed, not one seemed as anxious as I to search for causes of her husband's sudden departure. Some of the wives were too devastated to ask questions; others seemed captives of a female tendency to blame themselves; and still others seemed to feel that any attempt at explanation would minimize the reality of their husbands' unconscionable betrayal.

My intuition told me that Arthur's rejection of me was part of a massive emotional emergency—identity crisis seemed like a tame description for what felt like an emotional earthquake—and that his anger was fed by terror. My own background in psychology, a master's degree and experience with testing and diagnosis, advised me that there had to be an explanation for this upheaval in his personality and that environment was a bigger player than heredity. I needed to examine the possibility that the stress of the financial crisis had somehow unleashed emotional chaos left over from his childhood.

This was something of a Sherlock Holmes type of enterprise. When there is evidence that murder victims died under similar circumstances, it's reasonable to hypothesize that one killer is responsible. A similar deduction is made when a group of people are found to be showing the same symptoms of disease. All of these husbands canceling their marriages in such a hasty, despising way suggested to me that they might have been suffering from a common marriage-destroying malady.

As I investigated various clues, three groups of informants were indispensable; the wives who reported such similar experiences with rejection; the therapists who reported matching behavior on the part of their patients; and the authors of psychoanalytic texts who conduct their readers through the labyrinth of unconscious behavior and illuminate what is most mysterious about human behavior—our propensity for acting against our own best interests.

The first cue that I was an actor in a drama that had been played before came from the noncommittal psychoanalysts I approached immediately after Arthur's "announcement." They couldn't wait to get me off the phone and out of their offices—as if I were reporting symptoms of a communicable disease. Their instant pessimism after hearing my story made me suspicious that they were withholding information.

They were unanimous in their advice: Stay away from Arthur; get treatment for yourself. "But my husband is willing to attend therapy sessions. Why won't you invite him?" Silence, change of subject.

I persisted. "If his crisis is related to feeling unloved or unvalued, doesn't he need reassurance from the people who love him?"

"We can't interfere with his therapist," they answered with one voice.

"What if he's suicidal?" "Leave that to his therapist."

Among the dissemblers was a woman analyst I counted among my closest friends. But her reaction was far from what mine would have been if a friend called in such distress. She did not rush over to commiserate, and she didn't explain that something catastrophic was happening to Arthur. Her phone instructions were curt: Keep away from Arthur and don't question his therapist.

Within a few days she had convinced our children that I should neither inquire about Arthur's new persona nor seek a therapist to help the family. Her prescription—individual treatment for all five of us—seemed calculated to maximize the expense and the alienation.

After I had conducted my own sleuthing, I asked this same friend to confirm my suspicion that there actually was a syndrome of sudden rejection followed by sudden rage. While still maintaining that these crises are the private preserve of patient and analyst, she did enlighten me by describing a patient she was treating at the time, a woman who was having an affair with a married man. "She is becoming increasingly angry at him, but he is really a stand-in for a host of personal frustrations. I think she is about to blow her fuse and explode all over him."

"What would you do," I asked innocently, attempting to lay a trap for my friend, "if the man under attack were her husband? Would you give him any help if he called you in distress?"

"Absolutely not. That would be disloyal to my patient."

My friend was not about to change her mind just because she was sitting opposite a distraught specimen of rejection, but at least she had supplied an example of a woman turning on her intimate partner and of a therapist witnessing a number of these crises and likening the sudden eruption of anger to blowing a fuse.

While therapists write prodigiously about their cases, it is not surprising that the preponderance of their writing seems intended either to illustrate a theory or describe a successful course of treatment. When working with an individual, the "success" often consists of helping a patient leave a constricting marriage. It is understandable that therapists would not rush into print to describe involvement with a patient who is attacking his or her family. As I was halfway out the door of one therapist's office, she tacitly acknowledged that she had played a role in encouraging patients to move on to new relationships after rejecting their husbands or wives. "There is just too much guilt for them to go back to their spouses," she explained.

Much later I met psychoanalysts who didn't shy away from discussing the syndrome and who would have been willing to treat the family together in those crucial early months, but in the beginning I was inexperienced at interviewing prospective therapists and reluctant to broadcast news of Arthur's departure, hoping it would be temporary.

Exasperated as I was with the psychoanalysts, the visits to therapists of other persuasions were even more frustrating. They were disbelieving and bewildered. "Your husband couldn't be so mad at you if you hadn't done something to provoke it," said one couples therapist. Another psychologist was well acquainted with what she termed the "pop and dump" pattern—exploding and blaming the wife—but viewed it as one of life's curiosities.

In my quest for professional help, I must have paid about thirty therapists for advice and discussed my case with another thirty. Of those sixty, about forty-five were psychoanalysts. Those I visited in the first six months, before I tapped my friend Betsy, practically evicted me from their offices. The exception, of course, was Mrs. S, who accepted us for treatment but was blind to the obvious signs of Arthur's phobia to me.

After Betsy fortified me with language, I was able to summarize my predicament in a few words: "My husband has developed bad-object rage with me as his object." After a moment's puzzlement, there would be a frown of recognition. Some therapists would be compassionate, would even share some insights based on experience with patients suffering from similar delusions. Others told me by their expressions not to say another word.

Most of these informants (even the ones who were hostile to my inquiry) filled in a piece or two of the puzzle. Two years later, in a class, I met a therapist who was willing to share all she knew about the syndrome.

From my reading I gleaned more information on the psychological defenses that fit the profile of a rejecter. Guided by a diagnostic clue dropped almost accidentally by one of the first analysts I visited, I started borrowing books with the words "self disorder" in the title and quickly learned that self disorders are distinguished from neurotic disorders by who gets blamed when things go wrong. Whereas neurotics tend to overblame themselves, people with disorders of the self (aka character disorders) tend to avoid introspection and to transfer responsibility for their failings to outside agents or forces beyond their control.

These traits are common. Many of us have a built-in preference for condemning someone else when things go wrong. The term *disorder* is applied when the behavior is extreme. *Everything* is someone else's fault; inconsistencies don't register. People who dedicate themselves to courting admiration, repulsing criticism, and denying dependency may fit diagnostic patterns that are grouped under the headings of narcissistic or borderline.

The Danny DeVito character in the film *Tin Men* succumbed to his self disorder. First, he lost his car to a vendetta over an accident, then his wife to neglect, then his job to imperviousness to consumer fraud, and finally his house to unpaid taxes; yet as far as DeVito was concerned, not one of these calamities was his fault!

What shouted at me from the pages of psychoanalytic theory were the revelations I mentioned earlier. Without wholehearted endorsement from our original families, it is hard to bestow wholehearted acceptance on our created families. As I read case after case of patients haunted by insults from their childhood, I began to understand that loving wives do not compensate for unloving parents, that hurts from childhood collect undigested and undiminished in our unconscious.

Alice Miller has broken with the psychoanalytic custom of obfuscating language to write eloquently and succinctly on how cruelty is recycled from one generation to the next. Every page of *The Drama of the Gifted Child* is a gift of insight to damaged children and a fund of cautionary knowledge for parents and spouses.

By way of contrast, I realized how fortunate I was to have been born to parents who supported my individuality and ceded me my independence. Probably the most significant difference between Arthur and me was that I was treated well enough as a child to have developed a "good mother" inside me, a voice that told me I was OK, that I could forgive myself for my weaknesses and failures. Absent a resident good mother, Arthur substituted a cover-up, a mask of confidence and competence, a false self that could not endure the humiliation of career failure.

Arthur grew up with no adult to confide in, materially well off, emotionally impoverished. Relatives have told me that his parents were enchanted with him while he was an infant but too self-engrossed to relate to a growing child. His alcoholic mother had an insatiable appetite for acquisition and a proclivity for temper tantrums, and his elusive father exuded a hollow, compulsive charm.

When parental love is not reliable, children will withhold trust from later relationships. Children who have to suppress individuality to win parental approval will harbor lifelong resentment over being forced to trim their personalities to fit the parental mold and will probably develop a permanent allergy to the perception of being manipulated. Independence is risky for these children: They have discovered that love and approval last only as long as they are following the dictates of their parents.

Alice Miller describes such a child:

> He cannot rely on his own emotions, has not come to experience them through trial and error, has no sense of his own real needs, and is alienated from himself to the highest degree. Under these circumstances, he cannot separate from his parents, and even as an adult he is still dependent on affirmation from his partner, from groups or especially from his own children.

Doubts about whether our love is valued and our work is worthy seem to implant an unstable internal fuse, liable to blow whenever our pride is endangered. The enormous exertion to maintain the appearance of composure may stretch our self-control to the limit and impel us to compensate by tightening our grip and control over others. Thus, the thread of rigidity and passivity that ran through the wives' descriptions of their husbands' personalities: "My husband was very stubborn about his principles." "It was not worth the effort to try to get him to change his mind."

The cruel irony was that my reading was raising my sympathy for Arthur's past suffering, but my irregular encounters were with a man oscillating between insecurity, when he would merely castigate me for "not respecting my taste in ties," and fury, when he would excoriate me for "the way you kept me under your thumb."

This highly motivated man with the talent to do well and the desire to do good had been laboring against a Walkman in his head that always chided him for being fraudulent, inferior, and unworthy even when his accomplishments were praised. Now his secret was laid bare, and five lives were in ruins.

In the literature on self disorders, I found endless descriptions of patients who resembled Arthur the Persecutor—erratic, hurt, raging at the world, inaccessible, self-destructive, blaming everything on someone else—but I searched in vain for a description of an Arthur the Protector metamorphosing into an Arthur the Persecutor. There was no information on a breakdown, on a moment in time when an individual's anger, guilt, and shame overload the circuits and the fuse blows and the fury discharges on an innocent other, like a wife.

Nowhere was it suggested that the erratic, loose-thinking, contemptuous patient encountered by the therapist might have worn the disguise a few months earlier of a solid, contributing citizen, capable of expressing loving feelings for his wife and children. And nowhere was there a hint that wives and children might buckle under such a bludgeoning attack.

I now suspect that these omissions flow naturally from psychoanalytic thinking. The assignment is to trace mental illness back to its unconscious roots, not to speculate on how a previous equilibrium could have been preserved. Spouses and children are shadows serving mainly as gauges of an individual patient's level of functioning.

Figuring out why Arthur's guilt, shame, and anger were spilling over was a cinch compared to figuring out why he was blaming me. Why had he become so callous and combative? Why was there no residue of his previous affection or sexual attraction? Why was he incapable of sparing my feelings or considering my welfare? Why was he *so* accusatory, as if I had *never* been a force for good in his life? Why after twenty-five years did he remember me only as the person who usurped his independence? Why on two occasions did I see black hatred in his eyes?

To attribute this attitude to misogyny, an underlying hatred of women, would be missing the significance of the chain reaction. As mentioned before, wife rejection includes overturning a previously stable, caring relationship. There was no cycle of abuse and reconciliation. There was no previous break in the husband's attitude of valuing his wife, children, and reputation in the community. For reasons I will try to explicate, the husbands become so angry with themselves that they literally can't stop punishing their wives and children.

A sentence in a popular book, *The Angry Book* by psychoanalyst Theodore I. Rubin, M.D., was the first confirmation in writing of what I was experiencing. He describes the process of "removing anger from the person . . . we are actually angry at, and putting it on a 'safer' or less threatening person [such as] the wife."

Gradually, guided by the elliptical comments of various analysts, I generated the answer to "Why me?" It came in two parts: learning first about unconscious mechanisms for transferring anger, then about unconscious equivalents for a wife.

The basic defense mechanisms we use to keep away unwanted self-knowledge—denial, displacement, and projection—were familiar to me from psychology courses, but the focus was always on people using defenses to protect themselves. I don't recall any attention to the luckless souls who draw the projections.

First, let me try to relay what I have learned about how these defenses operate to cushion us from insults to our self-esteem. Then I will attempt to extract from the wisdom of object relations, a branch of psychoanalytic theory, some clues that would tell us why a husband might entrap his wife to be the stand-in to take his rage.

Denial and displacement are with us constantly. My failure to "see" the drastic change in Arthur's attitude toward me from wanting-to-please to needing-to-frustrate was a case of my own denial.

Displacement is another common defense. It still pains me to remember the times I hung up the phone after hearing bad news and proceeded to yell at the nearest child. Afterward, I would apologize, and occasionally I would confess that my temper was triggered by an upset that had nothing to do with them. Nevertheless, they were recipients of anger they had not provoked.

Since I felt guilty and ashamed of my loss of control, this kind of displacement could be classified as taking place within my conscious awareness.

Displacement is more perplexing when it is unconscious, when the displacer does not know that the anger is misdirected. An example is our middle child's reaction to Arthur's departure. He is in such a state of fury that he can no longer carry on a civil conversation with me. He attacks me as if *I* were the parent responsible for the breakup. "You always irritated Dad by being late." His emotional intelligence does not tell him that a minor incompatibility could not account for the wrath and punishment that are raining down from Arthur.

To this day, I haven't heard Arthur complain about my real faults, and they are plentiful. As for my lateness, he is justified in feeling that his promptness should have inspired more punctuality on my part, but Arthur always seemed more injured—as if I were insulting him—than critical of me for being a procrastinator and being less well-organized than he. What seems to enrage him is the memory of a wife who didn't do everything his way, who occasionally persuaded *him* to do something *her* way. To me it sounds as if he is lamenting his failure to prevail over me, a repetition of his failure to prevail over his parents.

As for our son's anger toward me, I surmise that it is rooted in personal feelings of powerlessness and guilt. He is divided between two parents who used to be unified. Arthur now seeks him out as a confidant; I ask for empathy and support, a request that puts too much strain on him and that can easily be refused since my love comes gratis.

Like Arthur, our son rejects every suggestion that he is angry at me: He literally is not conscious of it. Karen Horney's work with patients in psychoanalysis led her to observe: "If hostility is repressed, the person has not the remotest idea that he is hostile." But nothing in that sentence hints at the frustration of hearing your husband and child insist in voices quivering with rage that they are *not* angry.

From other mothers in the study, I learned that it was not unusual for the children to find spurious excuses to blame the mother. In fact, the situation was actually grimmer in the families in which the children supported the mother, because the choice was often involuntary. Those children needed their mothers as shields. The love and financial support that had been bestowed from birth were suddenly annulled.

Whereas in displacement we dispose of our frustration by attacking someone else (I scold you when I'm really angry at myself), in projection we twist our thinking to believe that the someone else is doing or feeling what we disapprove of in ourselves (I accuse you of being angry at me when in truth I'm furious at myself).

The following is an imaginary scenario devised to show how these defenses work. The cast consists of Donald the debtor and Marvin the mail carrier.

Donald is a credit abuser who has accumulated a mountain of debt. Marvin is the mail carrier who delivers daily reminders of Donald's indebtedness. Donald's chagrin mounts with the stack of unpaid bills as does his irritation with Marvin for bringing him so much bad news. One day Donald turns his dog loose on hapless Marvin: He has found an outlet for displacing his anger.

As Donald's savings disappear, he begins to panic. Simultaneously, he becomes obsessed with Marvin as if Marvin were the bill collector, not just the bearer of the bad news from his creditors.

Donald finds he can get rid of his gnawing guilt by projecting blame onto Marvin, the messenger. Instead of admitting that he overspends, Donald convinces himself that Marvin is persecuting him by demanding payment for bills that aren't owed.

Donald is confusing Marvin not only with his creditors but with himself. Donald's unconscious defenses send him messages designed to ease his agitation. They tell him some version of the following: that it is Marvin the mail carrier's fault that he is drowning in debt; that Marvin is the spendthrift; that Marvin has a weakness remarkably like his own—a craving for electronic gadgets and a tendency to spend lottery winnings in advance. Thus, Donald keeps self-knowledge and self-disgust away by projecting his failings onto Marvin.

A variation on this form of hand-off is *projective identification*, which is a defense that involves recruiting someone else to carry and express the feelings that are forbidden to us. Donald might pick fights designed to incite Marvin to anger. This would take the heat off Donald in three interlocking ways:

▶ Donald could read Marvin's growing irritation (over this entrapment) as justification for his blind hostility toward Marvin. (Remember, Donald has no conscious knowledge of having baited the trap.)

▶ His overinvolvement (or identification) with Marvin would allow Donald to experience vicariously his own anger and disgust when Marvin retaliates with anger and disgust for the mistreatment.

▶ By planting the blame on Marvin, Donald can hide from the truth of his own self-destructive buying sprees. Marvin the mail carrier is his siphon and shock absorber.

In our hypothetical case, the projector merged his thoughts with a virtual stranger. If Donald began accusing his thrifty, scrimping wife of profligacy, he would be exhibiting the early stages of the delusional system that underlies wife rejection. In contrast to the mail carrier, who can phone the police, change his route, or stop deliveries, Donald's wife would have few options and would suffer major trauma if Donald were to select her as recipient of his projections.

Why, you may ask, did Arthur and the other husbands in the group project their despair and fury onto their wives instead of an outsider like the mail carrier? One answer is that we are more likely to graft our thoughts and feelings onto someone with whom we feel closely identified.

Because Arthur and I had been so close, I sensed at the onset that attacking me was somehow a substitute for attacking himself. I showed the following passage written for the purpose of clarifying my own thinking about rejection to one of the psychoanalysts I approached for information:

> . . . feeling suffocated instead of comforted by the closeness of his wife, the husband forms a new bond and gains some relief, even

ecstasy, but not sufficient to hold back the flood of self-hatred which mounts until it is discharged on that part of his inner self which previously resonated with feelings of attachment to his mate.

Although this particular therapist wouldn't comment on my thesis, she did lower her guard momentarily and advise me to read about *object relations*, a suggestion I acted on promptly by enrolling in a course. I learned that object relations is a branch of psychoanalytic theory that suffers from an indistinct, even misleading, name. However, it deserves to be as well known as the Oedipus complex, because of its power to reveal the actual wiring of the unconscious electricity that pervades our intimate relationships.

As a first step in understanding object relations, it is necessary to drop our association of the word *object* with solid things. *These* objects are thoughts and feelings. Feminists use the word *object* in connection with the tendency of many men to treat women as material objects designed to enhance them. The theory of object relations relates to the mental and emotional processes that underlie a more universal tendency: to relate to others less as autonomous persons than as reflections and refractions of our own personal fantasies and fixations.

For quite a while, I resisted using the word *objects* to refer to people because it sounded so impersonal, but this language, coined by Sigmund Freud, the founder of psychoanalysis, is the only available terminology to describe the nuances of our close relationships. *Object* is a neutral word that encompasses, under a generalized heading, people, aspects of people, and all forms of disturbing feelings. It is the only terminology that can be applied both to our conscious behavior, in which we normally differentiate between people and feelings, and to our unconscious behavior, in which people and feelings are merged.

The language of object relations is as cogent for specialists as it is elusive for outsiders. Most of what is written is intended for internal professional consumption. References to self-self object, part objects, split objects, and rewarding objects are meaningful mainly to practitioners of psychoanalysis, who are trained to reflect on the facts, feelings, dreams, fantasies, and delusions that emerge as patients describe their conflicts and interact with the analyst. A psychoanalyst would be applying object relations insights, for example, in observing that a particular patient relates to the therapist not as a whole person with strengths and weaknesses but as an idealized figure, an "object" that can do no wrong.

An appreciation of the wisdom of object relations can evolve from subjecting your own pattern of relationships to intense examination. Idealizing is certainly one of my weaknesses. I realize that in clinging to my perception of my husband as a near-wonderful person with few defects, I was blinding myself to the signs that he was devaluing me.

The seminal ideas that evolved into object-relations theory were developed by a group of disciples of Freud in England, the so-called British School, who diverged from their mentor in holding that our psychological growth is influenced less by sexual urges than by powerful conflicts in the feelings that emerge from our interactions with people and events.

A Scottish psychoanalyst, W.R.D. Fairbairn, observed in his patients, and no doubt in himself also, crosscurrents and instability in the intense feelings toward people we love or find very attractive (love objects). We tend to perceive the same lover (object) as attractive and exciting at one time and dangerous and repellent at another. Thus, Fairbairn noted that good and bad objects are not opposite ends of the spectrum so much as opposite sides of the same coin.

For purposes of understanding spouse rejection, we need focus only on what object relations theory reveals about the husband-wife relationship. In object relations terms, a new heartthrob is an attractive, exciting object. The inner picture we form of a lover, usually an idealized one, is colored by erotic sensations and emotional memories of earlier love objects.

For twenty-five years, the "me" inside Arthur's head had been the collecting place for rewarding feelings. I was associated with things that made him feel good—his good objects. But objects are not stable. So much self-reproach was impinging on him that the "me" inside his head became the collecting point for the pollutants he needed to purge. Unbeknownst to me, *I* was merged with his internal bad object, the fear of abyss that threatened his mental health, if not his life. *I*, as an object or presence inside his head, had become as frightening as a death mask.

Another major contributor to object relations theory, Melanie Klein, was a close observer of infants. She called her colleagues' attention to the signs she detected in infants of a splitting or duality in their feelings toward their nursing mothers. She felt that a screaming baby temporarily hates the mother for frustrating its needs.

Melanie Klein proposed that the infant's experience of receiving nurture and frustration from the same source sows the seeds for a lifelong conflict between love and hate. At one moment we long for the good mother who nurtures; at the next, we hate the bad mother who suffocates and oppresses us.

Since it is mentally impossible to reconcile these conflicting feelings, we cope by splitting off the threatening messages and burying them in our unconscious. We compensate for having minds that cannot entertain love and hate simultaneously by splitting the internal representation of the parenting figure into nodules of good objects and bad objects. The more frustrated our quest for a reliable love object, the more frantic are our efforts to cover up the distress that these conflicting feelings create.

One way the wives in my study learned that they were no longer valued as good objects was being charged with mistreatment that applied to their husbands' mothers, such as Arthur's condemning me for harassing him on the telephone. Before the crisis, most of the husbands had publicly acknowledged their good fortune in being married to women who were partners in creating a more wholesome homelife than they had known as children. "My husband was always grateful for the calm and caring in our household, a departure from the hysteria that reigned in his parents' home."

One explanation for Mother-Wife confusion is the aura that links Mother and Wife as internal objects. During courtship and early marriage, the husbands seem to value the qualities in their wives that are an improvement on the irrational behavior of their mothers. This admiration for their wives seems to last as long as the feedback on their personal performance is positive. As the external world turns less hospitable, there's a shakeup in the internal object world. Feeling enchanted with your wife no longer compensates for feeling disgusted with yourself. Suddenly, Wife loses her plus charge for representing a satisfying object, reflecting triumph over detractors, and is slotted with negative objects, those that carry the minus valence associated with being oppressed or manipulated.

Of course, mothers are not the only damaging parents. The neutral language of object relations theory helps us make sense out of a wife's being charged with offenses that were committed by her husband's father. One wife was dumbfounded by her husband's accusation that she had deserted him when, in fact, she had stood firmly by him through very hard times. It took a long time for her to realize that her husband seemed to be merging her with his father, who had abandoned the family. When you become tied to a bad internal object, you can be mistaken for someone who has no resemblance to you at all, even someone of the opposite sex.

Assuming that a husband's unconscious casts around for someone to blame when his self-esteem is eroding, why is his wife such an inviting victim? By virtue of her physical and emotional closeness, she may be the most convenient, available scapegoat on whom to discharge the toxins that otherwise would poison him.

Breaking physically away from a spouse may actually carry less risk than breaking mentally with a parent. Many adults who felt abandoned as children tell of nursing a fantasy that their rejecting parent will be magically transformed into the loving parent for whom they are still longing. It is hard to believe that a person might draw more comfort from such a fantasy than from the reality of a loving spouse, but that's what wife rejection is about—sacrificing the most expendable link in a weak chain of self-protective defenses.

A recent book on the enchantments and disenchantments of love, *Dreams of Love and Fateful Encounters* by Ethel Spector Person, is more forthright about love-hate reversals than any of the material that was on hand when I began piecing together information on the wife-rejection sequence.

Person has a name for the switching off of erotic and romantic feelings: she calls the change of heart from idealizing to disowning a lover "de-idealization" and duly notes that lovers in the throes of de-idealization have been known to attack with projected anger and seize upon their rejected spouses as scapegoats. Person describes but does not judge the polar change from attraction to repulsion. The fickle, de-idealizing lover isn't held accountable for the consequences of his or her inconstancy; instead, the burden is on the rejected lover to take the betrayal in stride.

> The lover may be rejected . . . long after passion has been institutionalized in marriage. The rejection may be abrupt (as for example, when the beloved suddenly announces she has fallen in love with someone else and is leaving) or, more often, gradual. . . . The impending rejection is heralded by a new tone of voice, or use of a given name instead of the customary term of endearment . . . in the beginning the slights are small. . . .

Person advises the discarded wife to act promptly to protect herself before de-idealization freezes out memory and sense of responsibility:

> Thoughts of escape . . . preoccupy the [de-idealizing lover] as adoring reveries once did. . . . He feels he is being depleted, perhaps even cheated, by the money, time, and energy he must continue to expend on her behalf. Matrimonial lawyers testify to the almost inevitable outcome of lost love, advising their female clients to settle early, while their delinquent husbands still feel guilty, because "no one likes to pay for a dead horse."

Negotiating a settlement while the rejecting husband is still in a euphoric phase is good advice for rejected wives, but most of the time they are too paralyzed to act so quickly. (Personally, I couldn't help but take exception to being compared to a dead horse.)

De-idealization has a benign ring, like the off-again, on-again romance in a Katharine Hepburn–Spencer Tracy movie. From the perspective of the abandoned lover who knows not of de-idealization but of blind hatred, the behavior would seem to deserve a more fearful epithet, such as *bad-object rage*.

61

If *Narcissism and Intimacy* by Marion Solomon, a psychologist-psychoanalyst practicing in Los Angeles, had been published a couple of years earlier, I would have been saved part of the laborious, piecemeal task of assembling the information on child development to account for the way early fears and insecurities congregate in the unconscious to reemerge as uncontrollable impulses that endanger or destroy adult relationships.

Solomon discusses the connection between a fragile sense of self and regressing under stress to levels of functioning that were appropriate at earlier life stages and bailing out with defenses like splitting, projection, and projective identification. A person in jeopardy may experience "a fear of fragmentation and disintegration or alternatively, inner emptiness and deadness" and may "develop defensive patterns that wreak havoc in their . . . relationships."

Having driven home the connection between being mistreated in childhood and becoming a rejecting spouse, it is important to note that not all abused children are prone to adopt this defense. Moreover, other neurological and environmental factors may increase an individual's proclivity for using projective defenses. It's possible, for example, that factors like the architecture of the brain may play a part in predisposing some people toward the wife-rejection solution to adversity.

If the brain is compared to a computer, then projections can be compared to a programmed default setting. When the question arises as to who is responsible for actions or attitudes of which we are not proud, the default setting will automatically answer with a "projection," a message saying that someone else is to blame.

One psychotherapist, Margaret Golton of University Heights, Ohio, took this view of the causes of a bonding crisis. She did not hesitate to confirm the wife-rejection syndrome when she was phoned by one of the women whom I interviewed. Yes, Golton agreed, there is a behavior pattern that involves mindlessly casting off one's mate and it could explain why her caller's wealthy, well-connected husband had walked out, charged her with ruining his life, and then pulled every lever to wipe her out socially and financially.

Although trained in psychoanalysis, Golton changed direction and focused on brain research and its implications for understanding and changing behavior. She ascribes the sequence of fleeing and targeting one's spouse to a "limbic takeover," an acting on emotional imperatives issuing from the limbic system, the most primitive part of the brain, where raw emotional reactions originate.

Galton feels that a person susceptible to such a limbic takeover carries a weak sense of identity and self due to actual physical deficiencies in the structure of the brain, specifically, a shortage of neural connectors between the limbic system where impulsive, emotional responses are generated and the right and left hemispheres where reason and judgment are centered.

"A person who lacks a clear sense of 'self' will also lack a clear sense of 'other.' "

Galton's approach to therapy focuses on devising tasks to help patients self-evaluate and build more and stronger linkages between the emotional and rational centers in the brain.

As my investigation progressed, I gradually found my way to other therapists who encouraged me to pursue this investigation. They were frank to admit that only a layperson would be likely to write about the wife-rejection syndrome because therapists would have scruples about informing on their patients' aggression against their families and would face censure from their colleagues for breaking silence on this particular form of intimate betrayal.

On the next page, therefore, is an amateur's composite picture of the chain of events, deceptions, self-deceptions, illusions, and delusions that can deteriorate into wife rejection.

This schematic suggestion of the psychodynamics of wife rejection is meant to serve as a temporary working paper to stimulate research. It's only a first step. Much more information will emerge if professionals will pool their expertise to study the way bonding crises develop and exchange ideas about prevention and treatment.

The psychodynamics describe the unconscious push-pull of a struggle to contain emotional conflict—a struggle that is played out in two arenas: internally, or *intrapsychically*, in the invisible interplay of the emotions, thoughts, and memories that give tension and shape to our inner life, and externally, or *interpersonally*, in our vis-

From "I'M ALL RIGHT" to "I'M LEAVING YOU": A CHAIN REACTION

SELF-DECEPTIONS

Surface message	I like myself. I am confident. I am proud of my accomplishments.
Unexpressed insecurity	I'm not sure of who I really am. I have doubts about my abilities and about whether I am worthy of being loved. Fortunately, I can keep those doubts away when I do well and am admired for my accomplishments.

TRAUMA — Death . . . illness . . . aging . . . loss of job . . . business or professional failure . . . wife seeking more independence . . . wife criticizing . . . child not succeeding . . .

Surface message	I'm doing fine. Nothing is bothering me.
Unexpressed anxiety	I feel angry, guilty, humiliated, scared. I may be coming apart at the seams, but I can't risk telling anyone.

FIRST SIGNS OF DISLOYALTY

Hostility . . . withdrawal . . . new attachments . . . rejuvenation . . .

Messages to wife	Nothing has changed in our relationship. I'm *not* deliberately trying to frustrate you. *You're* the one at fault for not cooperating with me. Don't ask me why I'm spending so much time away from home or why I'm involved in so many new activities.
Unexpressed fears	I'm having terrifying sensations of breaking apart inside. I must do something to relieve my anxiety. I'm feeling more and more as if my wife is the source of my trouble. She seems menacing. I must get away from her before she damages me.

PANIC ATTACK — Overflow of guilt, shame, fear, envy, anger . . . conflicting urges for *flight* and *fight*

FLIGHT: THE BONDING CRISIS—I'M LEAVING

Messages to wife	I must leave you, or, I'm leaving you because I'm in love (or have found a new passion or religion). I'm thrilled to have found my true self at long last. Whatever existed between us is over. From now on, I will please myself. I have no obligations to you.
Unexpressed fears and delusions	Part of me feels on the verge of panic, but another part feels exhilarated and relieved to have found this new passion. When I am with my wife, I feel as if I am suffocating. She overpowers me. I'm afraid of being invaded. I must get away from her.

FIGHT: IT'S ALL MY WIFE'S FAULT

Messages to wife	I was miserable with you. You manipulated me. You never helped me. You weren't right for me. I'm not deserting you; I'm doing what's best for both of us. You stiffed me. I'm not angry; I'm leaving to get away from being controlled by you. From now on, you can take care of yourself; don't expect anything from me.
Chernobyl effect	My wife is contaminating me. When I'm close to her. I feel a panic attack coming on. She keeps me from performing up to my ability. She could annihilate me. I must protect myself by staying away from her.
REGRESSION AND RAGE *"You deserve to be punished."*	Obsession with primitive fears and fantasies . . . infantile sense of entitlement . . . need for immediate gratification . . . callous disregard for wife's welfare . . . acts of retaliation based on delusion that wife is persecuting him . . . pressuring her to behave in ways to relieve his anxiety . . . acting on compulsion to punish and humiliate her and to intimidate her from claiming her rightful share of income and property.

ible interactions with others that involve them in our efforts to gain fulfillment and relief.

If object relations sheds light on the unconscious electricity that travels between spouses, then projective identification yields information on the circuitry.

Setting up a projective identification with your spouse is an interpersonal maneuver designed to compensate for intrapsychic distress. The projector tries to induce his partner to participate in an exchange of behavior to relieve anxiety. The inductee cooperates (or colludes) if the behavior requested satisfies a reciprocal, often unconscious, need.

The traffic in projections between Arthur and me had been mostly in idealizations, flattering each other and making light of shortcomings. With so much "good object glue" holding our relationship together, I was more than content to feel loved and protected by a strong male and to bask in his admiration and reciprocate in kind. Believing in his success and "goodness" had the dual effect of suppressing any nagging doubts about my own success and "goodness" and also of elevating my behavior to deserve the admiration.

Unconsciously we were both obeying the same traffic signs until we reached the intersection of the business crisis. For him to follow the signs to a destination indicating he was living up to his vision of himself while all those bulletins of failure were pouring in, he had to redirect the incessant surges of self-hate, envy, guilt, contempt onto a stand-in—me—his wife—the person who was tiptoeing around so his homelife would be as peaceful as possible.

The only outlet for this anger—so intense and so denied—was to try to detour it through me. His method was to do mischief calculated to frustrate me so I would explode, thus giving him a vicarious experience with anger percolating in a safer container. He might have gained some temporary relief if I had lost my temper, but I didn't appreciate being recruited to vent anger; moreover, I thought my job was to be patient.

His second message was even harder to decipher. He wanted me to stop reminding him of our closeness and compatibility; he really needed distance from me to confirm that "badness" no longer lived at his address, that all of his toxic wastes had been forwarded to me.

Having enjoyed twenty-five years of one projective identification, I was suddenly propelled into another, an experience not unlike turning into a one-way street and discovering that the traffic flow has been reversed. You're still driving in the "right" lane, but the cars are hurtling toward you.

Whereas I was receptive to the original projective identification that satisfied my self-esteem, I collided with the discordant content of the new projective identification. Without warning, my husband had retracted the rules that governed our relationship. His new instructions: Stop modeling the good part of me, the part I exhibit to the world. From now on, you will be living, external proof that nothing is wrong with me, that all of the flaws and weaknesses that trouble me really belong to you.

In other words, you will be my personal scapegoat. Like the biblical scapegoat, you will bear away my sins. Like the familiar scapegoat, you will be the innocent who is punished because the real offender is too powerful. Like the scapegoat who stands in for the bad object, you will be goaded to accept the bad parts of me I wish to discard and be worked over until you feel as besieged and defeated as I do.

For starters, I will humiliate you by flaunting my adultery; I will make you feel envious by lavishing gifts on your successor; I will jolt you into powerlessness by cutting your support; I will accuse you of every misdeed I commit so you will feel as persecuted as I feel. Whenever I feel demeaned, I'll find a way to torment you. My internal keep-away catapult will convert stabs of guilt into projectiles of blame aimed at you.

This is the most sickening moment for victims of rejection—when the rejecter makes it utterly clear that he does not care how much he is hurting. One of the women I interviewed described it as "like being caught in a vise." So far, this nightmare has been described to me by women only, but I'm sure that it's only a matter of time before a husband will tell of the dreadful moment when his wife let him know by word and deed that his claim check on her conscience was worthless.

Unfortunately, the people who understand what it's like to be caught in the vise of a new and ruinous projective identification are not the people who write and enforce the rules pertaining to divorce. With the best of intentions, lawmakers, judges, and lawyers have banished considerations of fault from divorce proceedings. It's called "no-fault," and it sounds fair, but it can turn into a license for the rejecting spouse to use the divorce proceedings to intensify the punishment.

For most of the wives, the arrogance and deceit exhibited during the divorce negotiations had the effect of blotting out the initial impression of mental instability.

During the opening phase of the bonding crisis, almost every rejected wife said she had considered—if only fleetingly—the possibility that her husband's panic was a sign of a nervous breakdown. However, those impressions were transitory compared to the indelible memory of unremitting selfishness and cruelty—behavior that seemed deliberate and under conscious control. If a stranger were to embark on a campaign of attacks and false accusations, we would suspect that he or she was suffering from paranoid delusions, but coming from one's spouse, the compulsion to punish seems like directed malevolence. Angela summarized it for all of us: "I thought his grievance bag had burst."

Rejection being too specific and damaging a behavior to be excused or minimized, it seems incumbent to ask why marriage is a breeding ground for this form of crisis management. This inquiry is based on the premise that men and women are too important to each other to settle for the distrust that arises out of misunderstanding about the divergent ways for compensating for low self-esteem.

4

Mistaking Your Wife for Your Enemy: Whose Fault? Whose Tragedy?

▼

In Leviticus, the scapegoat is loaded down with the sins to which the ancient Israelites have confessed and then banished into the wilderness. A wife who becomes the scapegoat in the circumstances of wife rejection is not so lucky. Her tormentor knows where to find her, what to say to demolish her self-confidence, and how to cut off her emotional and financial lifeline.

Real and scathing as these attacks are, I don't believe they are consciously managed. I don't think that Arthur is conscious of bombarding me with displacements, projections, and projective identifications to make me feel violated, insecure, and overpowered. I suspect that he can't stop himself from unloading those feelings on me because he is too emotionally fragile to face them in himself.

Parents of adolescents are familiar with the battery of indictments that seem to express a need to tear down mother or father as a prelude to asserting their independence. These insults can be tolerated, if not excused, in our children by charging them to their immaturity.

Compared to your two-year-old, who can frustrate you with his unbridled sense of entitlement, and your adolescent, who can inflict real wounds with animosity that goes straight to your vulnerabilities, your husband regressing to these stages is a fearsome adversary. He has lived with you long enough to have homed in on your weaknesses, and has contested in the marketplace long enough to be a master at disarming his opposition.

When the language of psychoanalytic object relations is applied to this situation, the mere substitution of the word *object* distances us from the personal suffering. A sentence in an article on the treatment of narcissistic personalities by Dr. Otto Kernberg, one of the most prolific writers and highly regarded thinkers in the field, refers to a "defense against an intolerable reality in the interpersonal realm, with a concomitant devaluation and destruction of object images as well as of external objects."

Without identifying the "external objects," Kernberg is telling us that he has known patients who react to a disappointment in their person-to-person (interpersonal) relationships by downgrading their internal picture (object image) of someone close to them and then behaving destructively toward the person (external objects) they have downgraded. Language that is so impersonal and detached lulls the reader into minimizing the human drama. If the passage specified that such patients might react with a relentless attack on an intimate such as their spouse or children, it would capture our emotional attention.

The whole arsenal of defenses is illustrated by what happened in the opening moments of the crisis involving Norton and Lisa. You will recall that Norton suddenly exploded in anger and assaulted Lisa. He pronounced her insane and forced her to accompany him to court where he attempted to file papers to have her committed to a mental hospital.

According to Lisa, her husband had seemed stressed over shake-ups at the accounting firm where he worked and over the decision-making in connection with the expensive renovations to their apartment. He was also showing signs of being jealous of their infant son. That he could do something so violent and bizarre suggests that he was decompensating rapidly inside, yet covering his anxiety with the mask of a person who is in command.

When his fuse blew, Norton erupted with all four defenses that are prominent in wife rejection: He assaulted Lisa physically as well as verbally (displacement); refused to admit that anything was wrong with him (denial); attributed *his* state of "insanity" to *her* (projection); and hurled accusations that evoked anger and insecurity and doubts about her own mental stability (projective identification).

The image of an "internal keep-away catapult" supplied by Betsy, the therapist who finally leveled with me about wife rejection, seems a fair description of the battering machine that kept firing blame at Lisa.

"All the time he kept telling me that I was crazy. After his attack, I felt like a refugee from an earthquake. I was numbed and frightened, and it was a struggle just to get through the day. I had to stop myself from thinking about the future because *nothing* I had counted on was reliable anymore.

"He would do things deliberately calculated to make me angry, like *encouraging* our son to eat desserts when he knew I preferred to keep sweets to a minimum. It was not completely strange to me to be treated that way. My mother was subject to mood swings: The only thing about her that was constant was that she would blame me for everything. My self-esteem was salvaged at school where I felt valued by my teachers who praised my work and instilled confidence in my abilities."

Projective identification is the psychological term to describe our attempts to recruit someone else to carry our unwanted feelings or unfulfilled desires. Sometimes these "transplants" are enabling and successful. A typical example would be a mother who, having been frustrated in her aspiration to become a ballerina, "guides" her daughter toward a career in dance. If the daughter has a dancer's body, musicality, and energy, and if she finds dance rewarding, independent of her mother's influence, the transfer of ambition could turn out to be mutually satisfying.

Attempts at transplanting our aggressive or destructive feelings inevitably produce high levels of tension and resentment in the recipients. Thinking that Lisa was insane may have temporarily relieved Norton of his doubts about his own stability. Telling his wife that her actions and reactions fit his description of "insane" was certain to have the effect of unsettling her so that she would behave in ways that he could diagnose as "insane."

In object relations terms, Norton's behavior suggests that he had substituted Lisa for the bad part of himself, projecting onto her the unacceptable, disowned feelings that he could not tolerate in himself. Projection would have helped to purge him of tormenting feelings that at the worst could have driven him to self-destructive acts. His fury at his wife may have been directed at the bad part of himself that she had acquired from the projective identification. He could erupt at his wife and treat her with contempt as a substitute for directing those dangerous feelings against himself.

In a book on marital therapy, Herbert Strean, a psychoanalyst, gives the following example of the operation of projective identification:

> When a husband projects all that he does not like about himself onto his wife, he receives much protection and gratification. He can feel that all his unhappiness is caused by something external to himself rather than something internal. Instead of feeling small, he can feel a certain strength and power in belittling his spouse. He can also avoid facing his own neurotic problems by calling his wife stupid, boring, or asexual.

That Norton would attempt to have Lisa committed to a mental hospital seems a worst-case example of manipulating a spouse to counteract emotional distress. He might have seized on commitment as a way of removing her from his presence while keeping her under his control or as a way of receiving vicarious treatment for himself.

I felt something of the latter in Arthur's attitude toward my therapy right after he left. He was very anxious for me to be in therapy. In fact, that was the single contribution he was inclined to make toward my "welfare." It may have had something to do with relieving guilt, but it also felt as if I were being used as an intermediary to make therapy more acceptable to him.

Of course, a clinical dissection of such fearful events never does justice to the personal agony. Lisa had loved and admired her husband and was both confounded and "invaded" by this terrifying person who had climbed into his skin. Nothing in her education had prepared her to diagnose projections. Until she learned about wife rejection, Lisa was convinced that she could get Norton back on the track if she could only persuade him that she was not mentally ill. It was very hard for her to grasp that an iron curtain had fallen someplace in his defense system.

And Norton is not undeserving of our sympathy. Before suc-
cumbing to wife rejection, he must have suffered immense emotional pain in silence. Underneath such self-protective cunning,
there must have been deep deposits of guilt and self-hatred. If only
he could have told someone how miserable he was feeling, he might
not have had to resort to projective defenses that would torpedo his
marriage and cut him off from his child.

Lisa, like me, would have been a good listener and would have
used her powers of persuasion to urge her husband to accept therapy if she had had a framework for sensing the level of distress he
must have experienced every time he fell short of his expectations.

Projections—unchecked assumptions about another person's
thoughts and feelings—weave themselves into most close relationships: friendships, partners, mentor and protégé, supervisor and
subordinate, idol and fan, politician and voter, therapist and patient.

A two-week stint as a juror at the trial of a man being charged
with a serious crime gave me a laboratory situation in which to
examine my own tendencies for projection. When I first glimpsed
the defendant, I wondered whether I could be fair to a person
whose facial expression bespoke cruelty to me. I wrestled with that
bias and decided that I was capable of directing my attention to the
evidence only. The conduct of the prosecuting and defending attorneys and the judge during the questioning of prospective jurors
was also reassuring: They all seemed diligent and competent, indicating that the defendant would get a fair trial.

As I listened to the testimony, I found myself reading into every
witness a personal interpretation of personality and character. To
this task I brought all of my accumulated experiences in forming
judgments of people, plus the baggage of unconscious associations
from all previous relationships. How could I tell what part of my
judgment was based on the reality of the witnesses, what part was
reaction to their appearance and speech, and what part involved my
personal projections?

As the trial proceeded, I sensed I was developing a prejudice
against the defense lawyer because he was ridiculing every policeman as if they were all imbeciles. I had to keep reminding myself

not to let my aversion to the lawyer's excesses color my judgment about the guilt or innocence of his client. However, when he ripped into one particular prosecution witness, I suddenly felt my blood rising to a boil. I was shocked at my strong visceral response until I realized that the young man on the stand bore a striking resemblance to my son.

By the time the lawyers were ready to address the jury, the evidence against the defendant seemed overwhelming. I felt safe in attributing my decision to the facts and not to the defendant's unfortunate appearance nor his lawyer's heavy-handedness. Nevertheless, I settled into my seat in the jury box prepared to listen objectively in case there was something I had missed.

I noticed that I was approving just about everything about the prosecuting attorney: his appearance, his delivery, his argument. Yet when the defense attorney stood in the exact same spot facing the jurors, he seemed oversized and invasive as if he were intruding into my space. I wanted to close my eyes; mentally I was shoving him away. Perhaps he seemed demanding because I was feeling guilty about my prospective vote against his client. I definitely was experiencing sensations (or projections) of being engulfed, which I doubt would have been the case if I had admired his conduct during the trial or had been contemplating a vote to acquit his client.

At the moment of a projection, we are not experiencing ourselves as separate and differentiated, but as temporarily enmeshed with our recipients, so that we are unaware of having assigned them motives and feelings that may have originated inside us and that do not belong to them at all.

Recently I attended a workshop in couples therapy. A woman named Grace told the group that she was disappointed that her husband declined to attend the class. Some members began questioning her about his reasons. All of a sudden, others intervened and chastised the questioners for "attacking" Grace. However, Grace assured everyone that she had not found the questions intimidating. The workshop members realized that they had been projecting their feelings onto her. Since the questioning had made them uncomfortable, they had decided, without checking with Grace, that she was feeling under fire. Momentarily, they were so

74

allied or identified with Grace that they thought she was having the same feelings they were experiencing.

Because projections inevitably flow back and forth between people who feel close in mind and body, they are major contributors to marital conflict and misunderstandings. In the process of becoming a couple, we cross some of the boundaries that separate us as individuals. Sex dissolves boundaries, as do the day-to-day interactions of living together.

The ideal tuning between a husband and wife would be empathy, a capacity for accurately reading each other's feelings. That kind of closeness is deeply satisfying. Empathy involves sensitive listening so that we continuously correct our misinterpretations. It is this feedback step that is missing from a projection.

Projective identification—efforts to get others to cooperate with our needs—are often at the core of a couple's or a family's tensions. Many theorists of family behavior speak of contracts or collusion to describe the unconscious message and response system that develops within a family. The psychoanalytic term seems more informative because it invites us to explore the unconscious origin of these contracts and collusions, and to evaluate whether they are reciprocal or one-sided.

The benefit of recruiting family members to be our surrogates, to take roles we reject for ourselves, to give vent to forbidden feelings, to fulfill our frustrated ambitions, is that we gain temporary relief from our conflicts and insecurities. Our individual psychological needs are played out first and foremost among the people with whom we live, our families. It turns into a system because family members keep signaling their unconscious needs back and forth to each other; our wants are never satisfied. Maneuvers to involve family members in compensatory activities or attitudes are never-ending and are handed on from one generation to the next.

Among children who are truant from school, there is a special category known as school phobics. These are the children who spend their days at home, not hanging out and getting into trouble like "normal" truants. It sometimes turns out that the school-phobic child has accepted via projective identification the responsibility for staying home to satisfy a parent, often the mother.

One scenario is a mother whose childhood experiences have left her with disabling loneliness or fear of being abandoned sending covert messages to her child that it is OK to stay home from school. She might imply that many dangers lurk at school or that something terrible might happen at home while the child is away at school. The mother would be inducing the child into truancy to alleviate her unconscious fear of abandonment. In the process, the child would acquire the mother's fear of the outside world and would accept the mission of caring for her.

One friend who had volunteered to read my manuscript kept reporting back that she wasn't sure that she understood projective identification. Examples and rewrites didn't seem to help. Then she phoned one Sunday evening, a note of *voilà* in her voice.

"I think I finally know what you're talking about. My sister called me four times today, each time to chastise and criticize me. After the third call, I became exasperated and then I realized that she was looking for an altercation.

"First, she accused me of not spending enough time with her, which is patently untrue; then she charged me with being a hypocrite. As I puzzled over the second accusation, I recalled that she had attended our daughter's graduation last week and had been effusive in praising her for the honors she had received. In truth, my sister may have been feeling jealous since there has always been an undercurrent of competition over our children's accomplishments. When she called me a hypocrite, she could have been projecting her own falseness onto me. The effect of insisting that I visit her today even though she knew I was busy was to arrange an excuse for finding fault with me."

When you can't resolve a disagreement with someone even after several overtures and an honest admission of your mistakes, and when, in fact, your best efforts seem to have the opposite effect and the gap of misunderstanding widens, then you might consider the possibility that you've been entrapped in a projective identification. The person who spurns reconciliation may need to keep you angry to avoid acknowledging their own anger at themselves.

What I am facing now is an example of projective identification at its most destructive. Arthur's personal and financial attacks seem designed to arouse feelings of rage and helplessness in me, the very demons that are lacerating him.

Some writers in the field of family therapy give the impression that families operate according to external laws of physics or information theory or cybernetics. They dismiss the unconscious (intrapsychic or psychodynamic) layer as if everything we need to know about behavior is visible. Object relations provides a framework for exploring the unconscious currents that draw us into these highly charged exchanges and for gaining the insights that will enable us to change.

Using the framework of object relations and compensatory psychological defenses, it's possible to develop an interpretation for behavior that on the face of it seems to defy reason and commonsense.

Insult one: A husband who had seemed happily married takes steps to dissolve the marriage without telling his wife that his feelings toward her are changing.

Insult two: A husband separates in haste and proceeds to invent and exaggerate grievances that are bewildering until they are decoded as projections—unconscious attempts to divest himself of faults he wishes to disown by attributing them to his wife.

Insult three: After abandoning, the husband acts as if *he* were the wronged party, the one entitled to retribution. While demanding separation/divorce, he invariably sabotages the negotiations with brutal pressure, intimidation, and obstructionism.

Having identified the culprit in these hand-offs as the husband who initiates the rejection and attacks with the projections and the projective identifications, it is necessary to weigh the "participation" of the wives.

A number of therapists interviewed for the study insisted that the seeds of wife rejection germinate over a long period of time. They doubted that an alert wife would be blind to such deterioration in her relationship with her husband and hinted at there being

something fundamentally flawed about a person caught so un-
awares.

I would refute that opinion with my impression of the group of
wives who agreed to be interviewed for the study. Their "blind
spot" in relation to their husbands did not seem to be insensitivity
or stupidity, but innocence about the reversibility of good and bad
objects and about the invidious workings of projective identification.

None of the wives painted themselves as blameless. More than
one postponed talk of her husband's cruelty to discuss what she had
learned of her own failings in the therapy that helped her cope with
the trauma of abandonment. I, in turn, wondered whether the
therapists were more comfortable convincing the wives of their
contribution to the breakdown of the marriage than admitting the
truth about the rejection syndrome.

A wife whose object bonds are constant has no framework for
sensing the volatility in her husband's inner life. Although I wit-
nessed Arthur being overly harsh with our son, I never knew him
to hold a grudge or carry on a vendetta. In the mirror of my mind,
Arthur's image was stable—a decent, warm-hearted, honest man to
whom I also had a strong physical attraction. In the mirror of his
mind, the image of me was distorting from partner to usurper of his
autonomy. Yet I couldn't imagine Arthur *mad* at me. I had always
treated him so well—and he had done the same for me.

If he had claimed boredom with our marriage, it would have
seemed outrageous but not deranged. Charging me with having
ruined his life was so patently false and delusionary that I knew his
switchboard was sending scrambled messages. Moreover, flagrant
omissions showed that this was no sincere change of direction. Not
once in four years has he said, "I'm sorry for hurting you" or "I
would like to do something to make it easier for you." Every single
contact has been an occasion to add to my emotional pain and
subtract from my economic security.

A fair question is whether Arthur the Persecutor was always
lurking inside the false self of Arthur the Protector. It seems to me
that if the Persecutor had always been present, it would not have
taken twenty-five years for him to emerge.

Dr. Willard Gaylin, the eminent physician-psychoanalyst who heads the Hastings Center, which specializes in the study of ethics in medicine and biology, reflected on the bystander role of the wives: ". . . what is happening is in a sense an 'acting out' of an internal struggle on the part of the husband in which the wife is often simply a victim of his frustrated needs."

I was gingerly explaining the topic of my book to a fellow participant during a break in a conference. "Oh, you're writing about 'wife-ectomies,' " she responded, not even pausing for comprehension.

"Did you think of that image on the spot?" I marveled at her quick wit.

"No," she admitted, " 'wife-ectomy' is really my husband's invention. One day he was ticking off the number of men we know who have discarded their wives, and he decided that what they were really doing was giving themselves 'wife-ectomies.' It's the surgical solution to a midlife crisis."

Wife-ectomy, wife rejection, object rejection, bad object, Chernobyl effect—whatever we call it—it's not a pretty picture. Yet, if this is something that can happen when men (or women) can't handle stress, it deserves to be looked at squarely and with sympathy. None of us is entirely sure of what we might be driven to do when pushed beyond our limits.

Whatever misgivings these wives might have had about their husbands, not one wife judged her husband to be less than a loving father before his bonding crisis. These men, who cherished their good names, would not willfully have engaged in the wanton destruction of their families. This is the wreckage of someone who has run amok.

There's an amusing song from *West Side Story* entitled "Gee, Officer Krupke" that gives voice to our ambivalence about "responsibility." The members of a youth gang ask for leniency from a policeman on the grounds of the extenuating circumstances of their miserable childhoods. "We're depraved on account of we've been deprived," they plead.

Just as we might sympathize with a child's disadvantages and still hold him responsible for mugging a stranger, we might acknowledge that a troubled childhood plays a part in a husband's becoming a wife rejecter but never exonerate him from mugging his family.

It seems to me that we all lose—husbands, wives, and children—if we allow our awareness of the syndrome and its disastrous effects on marriage to be used as fuel for heating up male-female antagonisms. For the sake of relieving guilt on the part of rejected wives, getting help for the families, and placing responsibility where it belongs, it is necessary to be honest about wife rejection. For the sake of improving relationships, it is necessary to tap that part of us that feels compassion for the weakness that would drive a person to such destructive acts of self-defense.

Until there is more research, there is no way of knowing what proportion of divorces are caused by the rejection syndrome or what the ratio is of rejecting husbands to rejecting wives. Judith Wallerstein, a leading authority on divorce, warns in her book *Second Chances* that we may be entering a new era in which more wives are abandoning marriages. Scanning the casualty lists, however, the evidence seems indisputable that at this time the majority of rejecters are men and the majority of victims are women.

Nevertheless, it would be wrong to suggest that either men in the aggregate, or any individual man, should be thought of as potential rejecters. Many husbands could no more conceive of evicting their wives in a crisis than I could have imagined turning on Arthur.

One husband-friend told me a bit about his reaction to a prolonged period of on and off joblessness. He said that he was tense all the time and the stress caused him to develop high blood pressure. "I knew I was very short-tempered at home and grateful that my wife was so tolerant. I loved and appreciated her all the more for her help and loyalty."

Another husband-friend confided that he became very depressed when his architectural firm had to be disbanded for lack of business. He began seeing a therapist, but credited his wife with bringing him through a very dark and anxious period.

The lesson of this study is that *some* otherwise decent, caring men (people) are capable of reacting to stress by rejecting their wives (spouses). It was not only the trauma that predisposed them to becoming rejecters but also the seemingly stubborn resistance to talking about insecurities and disappointments. To me, every family devastated by rejection is testimony to a communication disability being no small matter and a warning against becoming more remote instead of more inquiring when communication is disrupted. By holding my tongue, I failed to press Arthur to explain himself at a time when he might have been willing to examine his chaotic, contradictory feelings.

The fact that I was more emotional and talkative and Arthur more disciplined and reticent seemed to be evidence of our being well mated. Part of the satisfaction and joy of a marriage is complementing and compensating for one another. I introduced Arthur to the ballet; he showed me the wilderness. He took care of the finances; I managed the interior decorating.

If I had known that a man with Arthur's past was likely to harbor a tendency to cover up his feelings and incubate a rage reaction, I would have given as much attention to getting information on his thoughts and feelings as to providing distraction and comfort during the business crisis. But how could I have tried to save my marriage and family from an unknown danger?

If one of my oversights was failing to appreciate my husband's insecurities, another was failing to appreciate that losing the business represented such an encompassing defeat. Devoted as he was to his family, a shattered family was more acceptable than the self-examination that would have been necessary to come to terms with a shattered career.

I think there are a number of reasons why I have yet to interview a husband willing to reveal enough about a wife-initiated divorce to verify a case of husband rejection. Perhaps husband-victims are even less willing than wives to discuss the pain and humiliation. Perhaps rejected husbands tend to react by immersing themselves in their work. Perhaps rejected husbands do not allow themselves to focus on the enormity of the betrayal. It would be a grave emotional injustice, however, to minimize husbands' suffering on the theory that at least they are spared the financial terror attacks.

Yet even if several husbands come forward tomorrow to confide that the wives they loved and admired suddenly turned into abusers, adulteresses, and embezzlers, it won't change the gender imbalance. There are too many statistics on female postdivorce poverty and too much anecdotal information on women who are left to raise children by themselves or to face a lonely, impoverished old age to reach any conclusion other than that a disproportionate number of rejecting spouses are husbands.

Why this is so invites an inquiry that could occupy volumes, but if the reality of gender differences in relationships is accepted, then I think a disarmingly simple proposition can be put forward: that more men than women are hobbled in intimate relationships by a characteristic set of conflicts which, if unresolved, has the momentum to propel them toward a crisis in which they have to extricate themselves from an intimate relationship in order to keep up the pretense of being strong and in control.

Specifically, these conflicts are around separation, individuation, boundaries, dependency, and a superseding need to look good by concealing confusion and weaknesses of all kinds. Unquestionably, the social agenda for males in our society is one that both creates and contributes to these conflicts. It's possible that the physiology and biochemistry of being male foster personality traits that perpetuate these conflicts. It's definite that growing up with parents who don't support individuality exacerbates these conflicts.

Before adding up the pressures on males that might spill over and cause them to convert their wives into scapegoats, let's stop and look at scapegoating as a method of self-defense. Assuming that the biblical scapegoat was able to survive in the wilderness, he would not have suffered physical or emotional harm from being tapped as the symbolic carrier of the congregation's sins. When a human is designated a scapegoat, the blaming (or displacement) includes subterfuge to convince the victim that he or she deserves the punishment (projective identification). The fact that this behavior pattern seems to operate like a reflex suggests that it is imbedded in our nature.

Traditionally, unconscious defenses like projections were thought to develop as a reaction to life experiences. As research on brain architecture progresses, more evidence may develop of physiology being a factor in the overuse of projective defenses.

As discussed in the previous chapter, Melanie Klein's theories on the emotional development of the infant have value for explaining how mothers come to be confused with oppressors regardless of the facts, how infants come to adopt projection as a defense against anxiety, and how mothers get to be the automatic receivers of those projections.

Klein believes that the initial reaction of the infant to the environment is to feel persecuted by what is perceived as chaotic and beyond control. Since it is so common for adults to revert to a paranoid interpretation of the world as hostile and attacking when they lose control of their emotions, it does seem plausible that what is occurring is a regression to the very earliest response to anxiety.

Klein also suggests that babies in the crib defend themselves against an inborn fear of a threatening environment by projecting the mother as a source of the danger and then splitting the image of the mother into good and bad. The baby develops good feelings toward the aspect of the mother that is nurturing and mentally blots out awareness of the aspect of the mother that is endangering. This would be the first internalizing of a person as an object, as a gut feeling that does not correspond to the wholeness of the individual.

If you are persuaded by Melanie Klein's proposition that newborns have a capacity at birth for retaining and transforming emotional memories which later will influence close relationships, then it would follow that the way infants experience their first intimacy with the caregiver would color attitudes toward successive intimate relationships.

Should the perception of betrayal by the caregiver in infancy be reinforced by actual betrayal in the crib or thereafter, then the child would be conditioned to distrust intimate relationships in general as well as the system of justice that failed to protect a helpless child from all-powerful adults.

This scenario of distrust breeding distrust would apply to both women and men. There is an additional hurdle for males, however, in that courtship and marriage involve teaming up with a member of the same sex as the person who was perceived—accurately or mistakenly—as the persecutor at the stage of utter helplessness.

It's important to note that Klein's theory suggests that it is the *biological* dependency in the mother-child relationship, and not a conspiracy against women, that is the culprit in setting mothers up for scapegoating. Presumably, if men gave birth and nursed babies, they would bear the onus of being remembered as the persecutory parent.

Nancy Chodorow has examined gender differences from the vantage point of a sensitive reader and interpreter of major voices in the fields of psychology, sociology, psychoanalytic theory, and object relations. After amassing a great deal of overlapping evidence from the various disciplines, Chodorow comes to the conclusion that gender differences and intergender conflict emanate from the fact of life that reproduction and mothering are the exclusive province of females. Whereas women's early mothering creates specific unconscious attitudes in male and female children that give rise to "associating women with their own fears of regression and powerlessness," fathers' distance from mothering has the opposite effect: Fathers are linked in children's minds with idealized virtues and growth.

With the changing role of fathers in today's families, we may actually be on the cusp of dramatic change in child-rearing practices, with a corresponding change in attitudes toward fathers. (Perhaps children who have been nurtured through infancy by a father hovering, cradling, and carrying them close to his muscular chest will emerge from infancy perceiving males as the sex that endangers their autonomy!)

For the foreseeable future, however, it will continue to be the destiny of males not only to marry a person of the same sex as the caregiver most acutely identified with the spectrum of infantile suffering and gratification, but to discover in marriage that they have reverted to being dependent again on a woman, mortifying for males who have acquired high stakes in exhibiting independence.

Turning from attitudes that can be attributed to unconscious processing to those that seem to be influenced by social pressures, it's possible without trivializing an immense topic to glance at the physical and social experiences that are exclusively male and suggest other reasons why males may be the sex more threatened by intimacy.

Differences in anatomy can be a source of unconscious insecurity for both sexes. If female babies feel shortchanged when they discover that males have an organ that they are missing, then males must view females as a visual warning that penises are not necessarily permanent.

Added to these observable differences are the hard-to-deny biochemical and neurological differences. Most men are physically stronger than most women. At this stage of evolution, males still seem to be the sex that surpasses in spatial skills, and females seem to be more adept at forming relationships.

In the department of *Vive la différence*, we note that the mechanics of sex will always be different for men and women. Women don't have to fear impotence, and men never run the risk of pregnancy.

Some psychologists suggest that males may suffer more separation anxiety during the two- to three-year-old stage of shedding the close bonds to their mothers. Little girls are offered the consolation of separating for the purpose of growing up to be like their mothers. Boys have a different assignment, to separate from the person to whom they were closest during their formative years and emulate their fathers, who have traditionally been the more distancing and demanding parent.

From time immemorial, males have been under social edict to appear strong and hide their feelings; they have been bred to be soldiers, to bear arms, to kill on command, and to exile their feelings to win their passport to manhood. They have been steered away from self-examination and introspection, the habits of mind that help us integrate our thoughts with our feelings, forgive ourselves our failings, and sort out our strengths and weaknesses.

Males who have clandestine doubts about their strength and ability will cover up with pseudo strength and pseudo confidence and a "keep out" sign warning outsiders not to probe too deeply. Anyone who comes too close might discover secrets they are withholding from themselves.

Knowing how much I suffer from inferiority feelings when I compare myself with more successful peers, I think I can empathize with someone who is tormented with what could be called a "perfection complex," an obsession with being perfect or best. Chasing such an unattainable goal would be hazardous to mental health.

You could never be satisfied with your own accomplishments. One wife said her successful husband was simultaneously envious of one friend who had made a fortune and another who had made no money at all but had written a critically acclaimed book.

Social pressures that encourage independence and separateness may have the side effect of discouraging intimacy. Like all excesses, the chances are that the person who overworks at maintaining solid boundaries is probably plagued with fears of being submerged. Having staked their social image on displays of confidence and success, men may be especially susceptible to a total breakdown like wife rejection when their failures and imperfections are exposed.

Because it is not perceived as weakness for women to admit their true feelings, women are usually more at ease asking for help. Such a safety valve may seem like a minor asset until you meet people who dare not use it. Since I began work on this book, I have heard woman after woman express frustration and despair at being unable to engage her husband in talking about emotions.

When one of Jeffrey Archer's characters in *First Among Equals* is asked how he can be so calm after suffering political humiliation, he replies: "Because I can't afford to let anyone know how I really feel."

Deborah Tannen has analyzed male and female communication styles and concluded that men assign a higher priority to independence than women. In *You Just Don't Understand*, she cites an example in automobile etiquette. Men seem less willing than women to accept a proffered right-of-way if it seems to compromise their independence. Women "are less on the lookout for threats to their independence [whereas being told what to do] sparks automatic resistance in men, because they have been accustomed, from childhood, to preserve their independence."

Lillian Rubin, whose book *Intimate Strangers* is based on her casework with couples, characterizes male reticence as follows:

> [A husband] can act out of anger and frustration inside the family, it's true. But ask him to express his sadness, his fear, his dependency—all of those feelings that would expose his vulnerabil-

ity to himself and to another—and he's likely to close down as if under some compulsion to protect himself.

We tend to accept it as the norm for a man to be uncommunicative and as the exception for a woman to be unable to express her feelings. As women are judged more and more by their performance in the marketplace, they may begin to emulate men in valuing the stiff upper lip of a competitor over the emotional openness of a nurturer.

One of the most telling statements on "male silence" appears in a book entitled *Manhood* by Stephen A. Shapiro, a psychotherapist in New City, New York, whose interests include protecting women against domestic violence. Says Shapiro, "We must struggle to keep aware that silence is not strength but dread of self-discovery, of vulnerability, and of the incapacity to respond."

Later he takes up the issue of responsibility: "It is true that silent men are also frightened, but that does not excuse the lie, the mistrust or the damage caused by that self-protective silence."

That confiding and confessing have therapeutic value may seem obvious enough not to need further investigation. Nevertheless, James Pennypacker, a psychologist at Tulane, has conducted experiments that offer convincing proof. Pennypacker reports that indicators of physical well-being went up after student subjects were given an opportunity to express in words their unformulated feelings of grief or rage or guilt. Asked to write (or later speak into a tape recorder) about the worst moments of their lives, they poured out their heartaches. It was found that the participating students experienced immediate reduction in levels of tension and a subsequent decline in visits to the health service.

Pennypacker concludes that confronting a trauma helps people to understand and ultimately assimilate the event. "Once it is language based, people can better understand the experience and put it behind them."

Almost every wife in the group I interviewed looked to her husband as a source of strength and competence. Hindsight tells us that she was fooled by a disguise. It is easy to confuse the appearance of a strong exterior with genuine strength and to leave out of the equation of "strength" a capacity for admitting our weaknesses.

A person who is authentically strong does not have to impress with an appearance of being strong or engage in compensatory defenses that involve belittling and exploiting his wife, his children, or anyone else for that matter. It's hard to imagine a man (or woman) who is in touch with his feelings and secure about his capacity to achieve falling apart in this way. But a lot of decent, well-meaning people suffer silently with blocks to their feelings, doubts about their abilities, and pressures to store their good and bad objects in separate compartments that can disintegrate under stress.

If the women in the study are representative, they had developed tolerance for their husbands' shortcomings long before the bonding crisis. A credit line for forgiveness accumulates after living together for ten, twenty, thirty years. Most of the women would have gone the distance to preserve the relationship and the family. Felicia stated the case so poignantly: "If only he had asked for help instead of attacking me so virulently. I would have done just about anything to save our family."

Felicia's statements are typical both in commitment to the marriage and reticence about intervening. If one attitude typifies the women who shared their stories, I think it was that their desire for peace influenced them to avoid confrontation.

It's possible that some of the reticence was out of fear of disrupting the relationship on which so much depended, but it would not be accurate to characterize this group of women as casualties of dependency. While none of the wives earned as much as her husband, as a whole they did not lack for ability or accomplishments in their own right.

Marie, for example, is proficient in fields as diverse as mathematics, languages, physics, and earth sciences and is the author of textbooks on scientific topics and of general books that utilize her talents as a translator. Her impression was that her husband, Larry, admired her brains and assertiveness. "It was only after he lost out on the appointment to head the agency that he began to resent my independence."

Preparatory to his sudden departure at dawn, Larry had connived to have Marie sign over their stock account to his name. Once she discovered the foul play, Marie was transformed into a determined adversary. She describes herself as "a formidable opponent."

"As soon as I realized how I had been cheated, I vowed to fight for my share. Fortunately, I had no dependent children and enough savings to pay for a lawyer and travel expenses to the state where Larry sued me for divorce, a southern state which at that time awarded property according to which partner had title to it. However, I was fortunate in drawing a judge who adhered to southern standards of chivalry. He strongly disapproved of what Larry had done and awarded me compensatory alimony although not sufficient to equalize our incomes. The alimony plus the income from my teaching and writing barely covers my fixed expenses."

Cynthia is another woman whose attachment and loyalty during the period of hostility that preceded desertion could not be said to reflect dependency. Her architectural clients were less prestigious and her fees lower than her husband's only because she designed less costly projects such as schools and subsidized housing for the elderly. Compared to her husband, however, she was the one with the more significant reputation for being an innovator.

If it can be safely alleged that women are the sex that works harder at understanding emotions and relationships, then it should not be a surprise that some of the keenest insights about men seem to have emerged from writings by women focused on women. In *Toward a New Psychology of Women*, Jean Baker Miller, a psychoanalyst, tells us: "Learning to master passion and weakness becomes a major task of growing up as a man. But sexuality precisely because of its insistence and its intense pleasure becomes an area of threat, something that undermines those controls. . . .

"And here, I think, is the greatest source of [male] fear: that the pull will reduce them to some undifferentiated mass or state ruled by weakness, emotional attachment and/or passion and that they will thereby lose their long-sought and fought-for status of manhood."

Soul-searching is no longer the exclusive province of women. Men are beginning to look inside themselves to better understand their attachments and the reasons for failing intimacy. Mostly they want to verify their sentimental feelings and their remorse for destructive behavior.

An exception is Stephen Shapiro, who asks himself why he failed to attain his own ideal of mature "manhood," partly defined by taking responsibility in relationships, and answers that he was so self-absorbed with personal rage at his unvalidating parents that he stage-managed his relationships with women to be superficial and self-serving.

One morning an article that was a real eye-opener arrived with my newspaper. It had been dropped off by a friend who is also curious about the uncanny radar men seem to have for sensing an incoming emotional query and repelling it with body language before it can be verbalized. Frank Pittman, a physician–family therapist from Atlanta, dips into his own memories and corresponding memories from patients to give his best account of the pressures on males to grow up in conformity with the "Masculine Mystique" and how unequal many feel to the assignment.

> Becoming a man was not easy for me, and my adolescent failures of masculinity were hauntingly humiliating. It took me years as a therapist to realize that my experience was the usual one, that learning masculinity is a desperate often devastating ordeal. . . . Masculinity is won at such a price that it tends to be overvalued for the duration of a man's life.

Somewhat apologetically, Pittman confides that masculinity is a status conferred not by the physical attributes of muscles and genitals but specifically by the validations of older males, preferably a father. "Every boy must have a man who is rooting for his masculinity. . . . We'll do anything with a man, but we fear that femaleness might be contagious and we don't want it to rub off on us."

Masculinity, as depicted by Pittman, involves a preoccupation with external displays intended to impress the "male chorus"— daredevil recklessness, athletic prowess, making it with women.

Pittman pinpoints yet another source of tension between spouses. Not only do men depend on the acquiescence of women to pass a major test of masculinity, being able to satisfy a woman sexually, but it is common for men to live in perpetual fear of women's anger.

> An angry woman makes us feel insufficiently masculine (unless her anger is based on jealousy in which case the anger affirms the man's masculinity) . . . most of the problems between men and women are related to man's panic in the face of a woman's anger. . . . It returns us to our childhood with mom.

Assuming Pittman is accurate in portraying men as supersensitive to women's anger, then this would be more evidence of a subterranean fault line forming in the mother-son relationship and widening into a crater between husband and wife. How unmanly to be so afraid of your wife's anger that you would either withdraw into passivity or explode into violence at the first sign of it. You would naturally feel under the thumb of the person whose anger could so unnerve you.

The tragedy is that all of this subterfuge to appease the male chorus must be kept secret. Men seem conditioned by infantile experiences and social expectations to distrust that aspect of intimacy that involves allowing someone else to know about your true feelings.

Needing an intimate partner yet fearing intimacy is a classical case of a double bind. You could end up hating your spouse because you need her so much.

Closeness to your wife can feel wonderful until something happens to reawaken memories of earlier closeness that felt stifling. Alas, you can't talk about your deepest hurts with the person who's your closest companion, because you fear she will misuse your vulnerability as you felt misused in childhood. You will try to exercise control over that person out of an unconscious fear of losing control and because, unconsciously, you associate her with the mother (or father) who used to control you.

It is not that women don't have problems with intimacy, it is that their problems are less likely to drag them into a sequence of defenses that end in a bonding crisis and an all-out attack on their husbands.

What seems significant to me is that women are more inclined than men to seek therapy in order to explore their anxiety or dissatisfaction with their marriages. On the whole, I think a woman would be less likely to sink all the way into a bonding crisis and bad-object rage because she would tell somebody how awful she was feeling.

Still, we have to wonder whether wives will become more susceptible to bonding crises as they assume more responsibility for supporting the family. In the latter circumstance, a rejecting wife would be in a position to do more than emotional damage to her husband and children; she, too, could shut down the family's financial lifeline.

Another inescapable fact about women is that they are both victims and accomplices in rejection. If the wife is the victim of her husband's bonding crisis, the "other woman" is his collaborator. There was no shortage of women to provision these husbands through the various stages of wife rejection. Every unfaithful husband located a woman (sometimes the wife's "best friend") who had few compunctions about breaking up a family. Peers seem to be equally accepting of the men who abandon and of the women who benefit from an abandonment.

Until it is named and studied, there will be no way to assess how common the wife-rejection syndrome is, but there is already enough evidence to state categorically that every incident sends out alarms far and wide that love relationships are not to be trusted. A single exposure is enough to permanently alter one's preconceptions about fidelity.

Wife rejection is a grim picture, but it would be a tragedy if public awareness of the syndrome were to set off an endless trading of charges between the sexes. It will be more productive to think of wife rejection as evidence of how hard-pressed we all are to grow into responsible and caring adults and to fulfill society's expectations of us.

5

Sound and Fury Signifying
Bad-Object Rage

▼

If four years ago I had read the following description by Dr.
Michael Balint, a psychoanalyst, of a patient's behavior in a two-
person relationship, it would have made little impression on me:

> It is . . . a two person relationship in which, however, only one of
> the partners matters; that partner's wishes and needs are the only
> ones that count and must be attended to; [partner two], though felt
> to be immensely powerful, matters only in so far as he [she] is willing
> to gratify the first partner's needs and desires or decides to frustrate
> them; beyond this, [partner two's] personal interests, needs, desires,
> wishes, etc. simply do not exist.

Now it reads like a clairvoyant synopsis of the condition of a marriage after one of the partners has suffered a bonding crisis. That
partner has converted the marriage into a narcissistic union—an
arrangement for aggrandizing himself by depleting his spouse.

Unrestrained selfishness was as radical a change in my husband
as was his sudden decision to leave after twenty-five years and move
in with a lover whom he had just met. Once he divined that our
marriage was not fulfilling its purpose—it no longer pleased him—
there was no way *I* could brake his drive to renounce our past and
to cast me as the villain who had thwarted his lifework (at least
without the help of therapists whom I didn't meet for another six
months).

When I read about psychologists evaluating the mental health of spouses after divorce, I wonder whether they have a scale for measuring wounds that don't bleed. One woman attempted suicide, another took to her bed for six months, and a third collapsed in a mental hospital, but the majority were stoic. You would not know that their grief was unassuaged even after ten years. They groped for words to describe the hurt. It's not like mourning a death, because the loss can't be blamed on disorderly acts of disease or nature. It is your husband who has taken aim at your heart, your self-esteem, and your economic security. My radar picked up the most intense and lasting pain from the women who were most shocked at being betrayed.

It was the similarity in the opening scenes of rejection—lightning departures, absence of guilt, distorted accusations—that provided the first clues to a common but heretofore unclassified mental-health emergency that, for lack of a preexisting name, I am calling a bonding crisis. The clinching evidence that this is a syndrome and not random violence against a marriage is the similarity in the malignant conduct after leaving—a prolonged campaign of emotional and financial persecution, along with repudiation of all attempts to compromise or conciliate—the behavior pattern that fits the description of bad-object rage.

Let me reiterate that I don't think that every episode of a bonding crisis ends as catastrophically as the ones in this book. In the course of seeking spouses who had been abandoned suddenly, I met women like Priscilla and Eleanor, whose husbands left for periods ranging from two days to two years but returned contrite and anxious to resume the marriage. I interpret these reversals as suggesting that some people go through a bonding crisis but recover their equilibrium and lose the urge to scapegoat their spouses. Either spontaneously or with the help of therapy, they begin to feel less toxic about themselves and therefore under less pressure to project their poisons onto their spouses.

Here it is necessary to dwell on the worst-case scenarios, the women and children whose lives were shattered when bad-object rage became a resident demon in the mind of their husband or father. To illustrate, I will try to capture the postabandonment biographies of Angela, Diane, and Kathy.

Angela's Story

Mark moved out the day after he told Angela that the reason he hadn't spoken to her since her return from the hospital to recover from her hysterectomy was that he had made up his mind to leave and had already retained a lawyer to handle the divorce.

Angela's friends rallied to help her through her ordeal. "More than once, I awoke in the middle of the night screaming and hysterical. I called a friend who lived nearby and she came right over. I was in terror: It was as if there had been an earthquake and I didn't know when the ground would start shaking again."

Although Angela had been the decision-maker in the family, she was no longer the money-maker. Her artistic talent brought her a highly paid job in the fifties, when it was rare for women to command decent salaries. Her salary had supported Mark through his last year in medical school and all of his internship and residency, and savings from her salary had comprised the down payment on their splendid house.

Only a few months before his sudden departure, mutual friends heard Mark speak openly of his warm feelings for Angela. After a dinner they had all enjoyed together, Mark turned to Angela affectionately and told her that he loved her very much and felt lucky to be married to her.

These endearments contrasted sharply with the scorn he heaped on her after his announcement. "He said that he had never loved me and that he had been planning a divorce from 'day one.' "

(Backdating is a common theme in rejection. "I was never happy." "I never loved you." "I've been miserable every day for thirty-two years." The words have the ring of fraud, but deliver pain commensurate with a third-degree burn.)

One of Mark's persistent post-departure complaints was that Angela hadn't "helped" him. "I thought he was referring to my decision to stop working and concentrate on running the home and raising our children after his medical practice was established. His memory was blank when I reminded him of my contribution to his education and to holding up the social obligations that came with his practice."

Before writing up Angela's experience, I went back for a last interview. I wanted to know more about the twenty-four-hour period between Mark's announcement and his actual departure. She recalled an impression which she had never mentioned before, and which, therefore, had not influenced my thinking about wife rejection.

"From the moment Mark started haranguing me, I sensed that he was really talking to his mother, who had always been resentful of me. While he was growing up, Mark took the brunt of her petty criticism and possessiveness. After we were married, she was explicit in disapproving of every move I made. I always felt that her real grievance was my taking away her 'beloved' son.

"As he was reciting my faults and denouncing our marriage, Mark was looking at me in such a distracted way that I had the image that he had pasted a picture of his mother on my face. Stricken as I was, it occurred to me that he was actually speaking to his mother when he accused *me* of never helping him.

"Something in his expression also gave me a premonition that I would never be able to talk to him again."

Angela's "premonition" took me aback. In the opening moments Angela foresaw the full import of rejection: that she would never again be able to hold a reasonable conversation with her husband.

I wondered why finality was so far from my mind when Arthur made his announcement. My thoughts returned to the scene at the restaurant, and I realized what *I* had missed. Arthur wasn't looking at me at all. The picture he had superimposed on my face was a *blank*. He was so enraptured with his miracle cure—a new lover— that he had simply erased me.

Angela and I were both reconstructed as bad objects but in a different order. Arthur recruited a new woman to replace me as his good object before he reassigned me as bad object. Mark fixed on Angela as his bad object, separated from her, and then filled the vacancy.

Angela didn't have much time for reflection.

"With my life plunged into chaos, I wasn't giving much thought to Mark's mother. He was finished with *our* marriage and was sounding as if he had liberated himself from a battle-ax. As for the episode with the dirty laundry, it made no sense at all. I couldn't imagine how my throwing dirty laundry in his direction could translate into a dream that I was pointing a gun at him.

"At other times, his non sequiturs seemed to imply that I might injure him. There were confusing remarks that seemed to tie me in with his mother as someone who might harm him by repeating the pattern that had driven his father to commit suicide. He also sounded a warning that *both* of us could end up like his father, committing suicide in our forties.

"It was hard for me to take these comparisons seriously, since I wasn't at all like his mother. Mark couldn't wait to get away from her. He felt that she had never liked or supported him. Although I never rated myself the world's greatest wife or mother, I knew that our family life was paradise compared to his.

"Our marriage was definitely not a 'ten.' I felt that Mark was very blocked and that he allowed people to step on him. He let me manage by default, and I didn't entirely respect him for that. My worry was that he would develop an ulcer because he was so self-effacing and easily exploited.

"Whatever my discontents, I had every intention of living out my life with Mark and our children. Our marriage and family life were as satisfactory as those of most of our friends. Mark seemed devoted to me and the boys. He was a good doctor and wonderfully energetic when he dived into a project. While he had his faults, I couldn't ignore that I had mine, also."

After his sudden departure, information on Mark filtered back to Angela through friends and from Mark himself when they met for periodic discussions, "which always deteriorated into personal attacks on me." News of his affair with his secretary arrived through the grapevine, as did the change of address when they set up housekeeping together.

Reflecting on Mark's character, Angela said she had always suspected that he was covering up a multitude of insecurities.

"Mark was more dependent on me than he would acknowledge. I felt that he had given me permission to be the lead partner while retaining veto power for himself. He was very skilled at applying the brakes and blocking what didn't please him. When I described

Mark's obstructionist tactics to my therapist, she diagnosed him as passive-aggressive. She pointed out that his habit of waiting for me to make up my mind and then criticizing my decision was a substitute for overt hostility."

Unlike wives who were shocked at being charged with "domination," Angela reacted self-consciously to this criticism. She had been the managing partner, and her impression that Mark preferred that arrangement did not alter the fact that what he complained of was partly true.

"There was something so childish and whining about his self-pity. He portrayed himself as a victim. If he felt so overpowered, why didn't he declare himself earlier? Why didn't he become more of a leader?"

The more I thought about the allegations of husbands like Arthur or Mark that they had been dominated, controlled, or manipulated by wives like me, who bowed to their assertiveness, or like Angela, who would have welcomed more participation, the more I began to suspect that a charge of "manipulation" serves as an all-purpose complaint.

We all use strategies for getting our way. Whether our methods deserve to be classified as manipulation or persuasion or trade-offs really depends on the degree to which one party is taking unfair advantage of the other. When the more powerful partner is one who cries "manipulation," the self-pity sounds like an escape via projection.

My husband's variation was particularly deceptive. Included in his expanded list of complaints was a new appraisal of what had gone wrong with his life. His mistake was "allowing other people to manipulate [him]." This seemed like a tortured route to responsibility—accepting and divesting in the same breath. About six months later, Arthur's grievance crystallized into self-contempt for having allowed himself to be manipulated by *one* person only—me.

This kind of accusation has a persecutory spin—somebody outside is in control of my life . . . I am not responsible for my failings and my false starts . . . outsiders are dominating me . . . outsiders are keeping me from succeeding.

Alice Miller traces supersensitivity to manipulation back to the child's experience of being made to feel shame or guilt by the parents for refusing to accept the role the parents have unconsciously cast them in.

Depression was the mental-health problem Mark acknowledged. A psychiatrist colleague-friend whom he consulted prescribed an antidepressant drug.

After abandoning Angela, Mark paid another visit to the same psychiatrist and gave Angela his version of the conversation.

"I don't know precisely what Mark told him, but probably some version of how 'wonderful' he was feeling, more or less what he was telling our friends. According to Mark, his psychiatrist-friend gave him the opinion he wanted to hear. He endorsed Mark's decision to leave me on the grounds that he was feeling so good about it."

Angela had repeated the psychiatrist's assessment to me several times before; her tone was always bitter. Here was a professional casually supporting a decision that "had demolished our family."

This was a rare admission of bitterness on Angela's part. In general, she reined in her hurt and reported Mark's latest atrocities as if she were describing the quaint, cruel conduct of a stranger. Her comic touch often filtered out the horror.

"I think my sense of humor helped me keep my friends, but it was gallows humor. Much of the time I was terrified. I felt imprisoned, like a fly trapped in a bottle. It was as if Mark had thrown a bomb at his family.

"I was in no condition to cope with our children's anguish and outrage. Our younger son, Andy, became alienated and depressed, and Fred, our older son, started hanging out with a gang of troublemakers. Very soon after Mark left, the school called to say that Fred's grades had taken a dive.

"Frankly, I was too stressed to be effective with either child. My biggest worry was whether there was going to be another check from Mark. It's very terrifying to be dependent on an *allowance* from someone who's telling you how much he hates you.

"Other than occasional campaigns to lure the boys to live with him, Mark gave them no fatherly attention at all. He closed his ears and eyes to Fred's antisocial behavior, which was very serious, and even made himself scarce when they had medical problems. I couldn't even reach him when Fred contracted pneumonia.

"Mark's hostility toward Andy—who was more allied with me—bordered on abuse. Just recently I learned how unwelcome Mark had made him feel. When Andy stayed with his father and his secretary-turned-mistress while I was away for a few weeks, he had to sleep on a makeshift bed consisting of two dining-room chairs.

"After the divorce, I had to go to court to force Mark to keep his agreement to pay Andy's tuition for his private school. Since his school performance had also declined after the abandonment, he truly needed the small classes and personal attention.

"On one occasion, Mark actually talked an ophthalmologist-friend out of prescribing contact lenses for Andy even though the cost would have been covered by insurance!

"On his sixteenth birthday, Andy received a registered letter from his father. It was no birthday greeting. Mark, who prided himself on being a graduate of one of the elite Ivy League colleges, informed his son that he would pay tuition only for a state university. The insult had the desired effect. Our very bright, talented second child lost his motivation and never attended college.

"Fred, on the other hand, eventually quieted down and shifted into an achievement mode, but he has encased himself in a virtually impenetrable shell. One child reacted to his father's desertion by suppressing his emotions in order to become assertive; the other child did the opposite."

As for Angela herself, the financial punishment was brutal. She used up her savings during the prolonged negotiations leading to the divorce. "My work experience was out of date and I was in a state of shock. I went back into therapy. In fact, I saw a therapist individually for help in pulling myself together and also attended group therapy in the company of several friends.

"The therapist for our group had an amazing intuition for sensing the source of family problems. She had only informal credentials—training in active listening, Gestalt, and Transactional Analysis—but she helped us gain insight into our own motivations and improve our skills for relating to family members who are angry and irrational.

"Those techniques helped me deal with my children and talk to Mark without going up in smoke at every provocation. Since Mark held all the money and power, I *had* to deal with him. My therapist advised me to get him to talk about his complaints and to take them seriously and reflect on the nature of the gripe, no matter how trivial, farfetched, or unjustified it seemed to me.

"The content of his complaints kept changing. The version he gave in my lawyer's office was truly astonishing. In the course of taking a deposition, my lawyer asked him to state his reasons for wanting the divorce. Mark seemed tongue-tied. The question was repeated, and again there was silence. His lawyer asked for a recess. When we reconvened, Mark cleared his throat and said, 'She read too many books, frequently fiction. And she did too many crossword puzzles.' He also mentioned *my* 'depression.' "

In the divorce settlement, Angela got the house, but the timing was very unlucky. Her alimony dwindled in value during the inflationary period of the seventies. She was forced to sell the house to maintain even the frugal life-style that was such a comedown from the comfortable affluence of her marriage.

After the divorce, Mark found another way to harass her.

"He never sent his check for the alimony on the date it was due. I had to take him to court to compel payment. No one could understand why a doctor would take a day out for a court appearance. Some friends thought he wanted to see me. I thought he needed to torment me. I cursed my lawyer for not protecting me better. Every alimony payment was reduced by the amount of the legal fee I had to pay to collect it."

I asked Angela the same questions I had asked the other wives whose histories became part of my study. Was there ever any hint in Mark's predeparture behavior that he was capable of the cruelty he showed toward you and the children? Had he ever treated anybody else that way? Was there a vengeful streak every once in a while, which you had discounted?

"I was definitely aware of being the target of some hostility and resentment which seemed to substitute for getting angry at other people who misused him, but I never knew Mark to abuse anyone, and abandonment was unimaginable."

Mark, of course, was the only one of the husbands whom I knew well enough to have formed an opinion about his character. During the fifteen years that we had a couple-to-couple and family-to-family relationship, I thought of him as a fundamentally "decent person," a caring doctor, someone who would never actively hurt friend or foe.

The only jarring note I recall was a whispered conversation at the dinner table in which Mark confessed that he worried about the tragedy of losing a child and wished that they had had a third child as a sort of insurance policy. This confidence troubled me because it seemed to imply a devaluing of the individuality of his sons, but I know it's not unusual for parents to want a third child as a form of backup.

Angela had the misfortune of losing a baby through a miscarriage in her late thirties, and then, several years later, there was the hysterectomy, which may have pushed Mark over the edge into a bonding crisis. Knowing of his wish for another child, I could imagine his experiencing disappointment, even resentment, toward Angela for involuntarily canceling his hopes, but nothing I ever saw or heard hinted that this was a man capable of carrying on a permanent vendetta against the wife and children of whom he had seemed so proud.

You might speculate that these half-hidden, half-expressed fears of death and suicide had set Angela up for the Chernobyl effect, or you might depict the sudden personality change in object relations terms. Unconsciously, Mark seemed to have reacted to a large quantum of anxiety by evicting his wife and children from the compartment containing his good objects and transferring them into a compartment with his bad objects, the pieces of himself that had to be sacrificed in an attempt to contain his distress.

Diane and Nick

The friend who introduced me to Diane described her as still very wounded and unreconciled to her husband's defection to a homosexual relationship.

I spent the afternoon at her sprawling suburban home. Five years had passed since the night at the restaurant when Nick announced his affair, yet the details of the financial settlement were still being worked out.

Diane herself put a warning label on her story. "My experience is too scary for most people to tolerate. I hadn't a clue that anything was wrong with our marriage or that my husband was bisexual. We were known as an ideal couple. The thought that a spouse could change on a dime is just too unnerving.

"I always assumed that a man who became homosexual could not have been truly heterosexual in the first place. I'm afraid that isn't true. Sex is not a subject I am inclined to discuss with a stranger, but I will say that Nick seemed every bit as contented with our marriage and sex life as I was.

"Frankly, it is as shocking to experience a drastic change in your husband's personality as in his sexual orientation. From a partner who seemed to think better of me than I did of myself, he turned into an ex-partner with a compulsion to do every form of mischief to me.

"While I have felt invaded by the amount of scrutiny that has accompanied his exodus, there has also been some sharing of confidences. So many women have confided that the sex in their marriage was only 'so-so.' I felt the opposite, and Nick always talked and acted as if he found the physical side of our relationship a strong contributor to our compatibility. I could have imagined our marriage suffering if either of us had developed a physical disability that interfered with sex.

"His conversion occurred just when AIDS was being diagnosed, so it seemed like a terribly self-destructive course to take. When he told me his news, he sounded as if he had just had an epiphany and that he couldn't allow himself to grow one day older unfulfilled. AIDS didn't concern him at all. He said that his therapist had encouraged him to tell me about his affair on the theory that he could inform me without broadcasting it from the rooftops.

"At first, the only person I confided in was a therapist. She said that if he had been her patient, she never would have handled the problem that way. She would have tried to help him work through his sexual confusion without revealing it to his wife. She definitely thought that honesty could be postponed in a situation like this."

"Had you met your husband's therapist?" I asked.

"No, Nick had told me that he had decided to see a therapist a few months before. I thought it was a good idea because he needed to tell someone about his professional disappointments, and he had declared the subject off limits between us.

"It was unlike him to be so secretive about who he was seeing, but I thought it best not to intrude. It turned out that his therapist was something of a phony because he did not have the graduate degrees he claimed. It actually took Nick, who was meticulous about insurance and reimbursement, four months to discover that his insurance would not cover the fees of an unaccredited therapist.

"I wasted more time and money trying to get information from therapists than I care to estimate. Therapists see so much outlandish conduct that *nothing* seems to surprise them. All sorts of theories were offered: that the homosexual affair was a way to get back at his father, that he had never really liked women. What seems plausible to me is that sexual orientation, which I took to be a property of hormonal makeup, must also have a lot to do with identity. I told him immediately that I thought the change was in his head, not in his hormones, but once he believed he was homosexual or bisexual, it was a reality.

"My fantasy was that the change could be reversed if someone would just tell him he was mistaken, that even if he had struggled with some fear about homosexuality, his true self was the one I had lived with for twenty-six years. It also occurred to me that he might benefit from facing that part of himself that was under cover and that he would become a more integrated person for doing so. That's just a small sample of my naïveté."

"Were there no hints about his bisexuality?" I asked.

"Not from the way he behaved toward me as a woman. But there were a multitude of signs of an affair with a male that preceded the one that ended our marriage which I was too dense to notice.

"After first being passed over for the promotion and then rejected by the search committee for the executive position that would have redeemed his career, he began spending more time than seemed appropriate with his young male assistant. I didn't think his assistant was sufficiently talented to warrant so much attention from Nick nor was I very cordial, because I felt that he was drawing off some of the mentor relationship that belonged to our sons.

"Nick would ask me to include his assistant in family occasions, and I would object strenuously. I sensed that the relationship was unhealthy and that it filled a niche that was compensatory for his professional setbacks, but it never crossed my mind that it was sexual. If he had been trying to insinuate a female assistant into the household, I'm sure I would have been more suspicious.

"Everything is so obvious now that it is hard to re-create the time when I simply was not finding fault with my husband. Despite the discord over his assistant, I loved and trusted him."

"Was there a decline in your sexual relationship?" I asked.

"Not really. There was a drop in our affectionate relationship, like not holding hands in the movies or taking romantic walks under the stars. I would tell him that I loved him with my usual frequency, and I guess I didn't notice that his response lacked conviction, or I continued to read in the sincerity that I had heard before.

"I learned in therapy that my blindness was really denial. When I told my therapist that we had never had a serious quarrel, she looked at me askance as if to say, 'You fool. Who doesn't know that so much peace is unnatural; it's a danger sign in a marriage. Somebody's holding back.'

"I did realize that something was amiss, but I couldn't imagine Nick changing his mind about our marriage, after so much approval over so many years. He was always affirmative about us, and nothing had happened to change that. I felt that we would get back on track as soon as his professional situation stabilized. There I was faithfully trying to boost his ego, and all the while he was drifting away."

"Were there other incidents that you overlooked?"

"Well, I was hurt and mystified by his absenting himself from the funeral of one of my favorite cousins. This was strange neglect because he had always been attentive to me, and to my family, in illnesses and emergencies.

"There was also a new pattern of blocking my preferences. For example, we needed to change the wallpaper in the dining room. I kept bringing home samples of papers that I thought were terrific, and he would veto them, so I tried to get him to come with me to speed the process, but he resisted. It seemed perverse, as if he wanted a stalemate. In fact, I think he's still talking to the children about our incompatibility over the wallpaper.

"Nick seemed to be fixating on unnecessary home improvements and obstinately refusing to cooperate with any changes I proposed."

"Was he putting up barriers because money was short?"

"No, these were small expenses that we could easily afford. We had not suffered a loss of income. What he had missed out on was the increase in salary and prestige that would have come with the promotion.

"After he left, he accused me of being extravagant. While I was never a penny-pincher, I was definitely careful about expenditures. His mother used to go on buying sprees, not me."

"Would you have been more or less upset if his affairs had been with women?"

"Everyone wants to speculate about that. Some people insist that it's worse for a wife when the other woman is a man because she feels so violated. Others claim that it's less awful to be discarded for a lover with whom she can't compete. As far as I'm concerned, if your standard is monogamy, *any* affair is a monumental insult.

"When Nick blurted out the news of his liaison, I told him that it really didn't matter whether it was woman or man: his being involved with another person meant that our relationship was no longer exclusive. You can't be in love with two people at the same time."

I asked Diane how Nick had treated her after he left.

"Since Nick had always been kind and generous, I expected him to be considerate of me even while pursuing this affair. I assumed that we would see each other frequently, and that he would be available when problems arose, and that our parenting would continue.

"For the first nine months, we met for regular lunches. In my mind he was suffering from amnesia and would get over it. I kept telling myself that until one shattering lunch when he looked at me with stony, hard-boiled eyes, like a Gestapo agent in a World War Two movie. The memory still makes me shudder.

"From then on I knew there was a possibility that he would harm me, but I really couldn't take any initiative to protect myself, like filing for a divorce. I was mostly paralyzed.

"Gradually I began to catch on that he was angry with me for being an obstacle to having his way about everything; he was really mad at me for being alive. He sent me letters telling me I had to move out of *his* house, as if *my* having a place to live was a detail of no consequence whatsoever. I might as well have been some residue of contaminated waste. Any disposal site would do."

"Was there a change in his relationship with your children?"

"Well, he really lost a good deal of his coping capacity. Although the boys didn't detect it, I sensed that he was faking his relationship with them and that he dismissed their problems because he really couldn't think his way through them. He had been the kind of father who was involved in every event in his children's lives and never skimped on attention.

"As each boy reached adolescence, Nick seemed to need to establish his dominance by constantly demonstrating his superior knowledge and command. He would react to mild rebellion as if it were mutiny. It seemed incongruous for a father to be so nurturing toward little children and then so intolerant of comparatively mild assertiveness on the part of adolescents."

"How have your sons treated you since Nick left?"

"Our rapport was suspended for at least four years. You would never have guessed that we had been a very close family. The boys would not discuss their feelings and really preferred not to talk to me at all. In order to maintain a relationship, I have to abide by their rules: I am not allowed to mention Nick's name. It took every ounce of patience and forbearance to restore communication. Just recently there has been a thaw; they are actually sending some affection and warmth in my direction for the first time in five years! The emotional losses from Nick's breaking up the family are incalculable."

"Are you worried about the effect on their sexual orientation?"

"Of course, but the damage I am seeing now is to their capacity for trust and discipline. Our older son had made high honors all the way through college until his senior year when Nick left and his grades fell to barely passing. He's still foundering, and I don't know whether he will ever regain the ground he lost. Our younger son seems to be clinging to a relationship with a young woman that does not seem destined for marriage."

"Does your husband tell your sons that he left because of his homosexuality?"

"I really don't know what Nick says to them, but I doubt that the change in sexual orientation is discussed. My impression is that he sounds a note of self-pity, bemoaning how *we* didn't get along, which ends up as a complaint that I didn't follow all of his wishes. When he says that to me, I ask him why he neglected to mention his discontent while we were living together, and he becomes furious.

"The reason I brought up the controversy over choosing wallpaper for the dining room is that our younger son has fixated on it as the cause of the downfall of our marriage. He has cited it at least fifteen times, so I'm sure Nick must carry on about how I overpowered him in the wallpaper department. He says that Dad felt left out. Our son refuses to know about Nick's anger and abuse, and the change to homosexuality is forgotten altogether. It really worries me that he can imagine twenty-six years of marriage dissolving over a difference of opinion about wallpaper!

"Perhaps the boys would have judged Nick more harshly if he had left for a woman. The homosexuality gives him the cover of having made a change that was beyond his control. However, it seems to me that an honest change to homosexuality would not have involved such blanket rejection of *my* humanity. I may be wrong, but I think he needed to leave *me* and would have gotten involved with another woman if some inner quirk hadn't steered him to a man."

I asked Diane whether she had gotten support from friends.

"Almost everyone vanished. About three friends have remained close and caring, and without them I think I might have gone under."

"Did your friends treat Nick the same way?"

"Well, he kept his change in sexual orientation a secret for about a year. People would ask him whether he had another woman, and he would say no. I'm not sure when he started introducing his friend around. Some of the people who have ignored me have been seeing him. It's possible that he has acquired a certain allure for doing something forbidden and dangerous."

"What has happened with money?"

"Nick kept cutting the voluntary support until my lawyer warned that it could work against me in a settlement if I appeared to be managing on the declining amounts he was providing.

"Since there was no question of remarriage, Nick didn't press for a divorce. For my part, I was reluctant to start a legal action and told myself that he would not stoop to anything too terrible for fear of alienating our sons. However, that protection proved illusory. The boys block out all information on the emotional and financial abuse. It is imperative for them to preserve their positive image of their father.

"I know that it is typical for a husband who has left his wife to cheat her out of money, but I thought Nick was too honorable for that. While there's not much sympathy today for the wife who isn't self-supporting, that wasn't the case when we were married. Nick's income supported the family, and that was the way he wanted it. I worked part time as a social worker so I could be available as hostess and companion.

"It isn't that I sacrificed to be a 'good' wife: I was very fulfilled being his partner and mother to our children, but it meant that I based all of my life decisions on the solidity of our marriage. If Nick hadn't made me feel so secure, I would have been watching out for my personal income.

"While I have no qualms about pushing my lawyer to obtain as large a settlement as possible, I cannot steel myself to face Nick in court.

"Whatever happened to our marriage was of his doing. He broke faith by never revealing that anything was wrong. He could have gone to a therapist when he first started experiencing conflict about his sexual orientation, and he could have shared his secret with me.

It would have shaken me with the force of an earthquake to learn about his attraction to men, but I would have tried to help if he had shown a particle of humility or desire to be loyal to the family. As it was, I gave him much too much time to rearrange his assets, so I will get only a fraction of my entitlement in the settlement."

Diane had never heard of the Chernobyl effect or bad-object rage, but she had formed a very clear picture of what it's like to be a victim of both.

"It took me a long time to pinpoint Nick's monomania. The words I never heard were 'I'm sorry to be doing this to you.' He has been on a self-justifying binge for five years, and it has cost him and me and our children everything we cherished."

Kathy and Alex

Kathy had always taken pride in Alex's ability and achievements, but he was not an easy person to get along with. After their son was killed in a boating accident, he plunged himself almost full time into their importing business. Kathy recalled that he seemed to draw some comfort from his music, "but mostly he kept himself occupied with the business.

"Alex had always embarrassed me a little with his perpetual need to present himself as the all-round expert. Now he needed to win every argument. He could be very overbearing, but people tolerated it because he was so smart and could produce on his self-advertising.

"I remember a dinner with a potential customer during which Alex spent the entire evening impressing our guest with his superior command of every facet of that man's business and never stopped for a moment to listen. We lost him as a customer. I was inwardly furious but said little to Alex because it seemed futile to tell him that I felt that his assertiveness was temporarily out of control.

"I knew that many marriages collapse after the loss of a child, but never imagined us becoming a casualty. The school principal actually cornered us at a Parent Association reception to warn us that the loss of a child puts a dreadful strain on a marriage. He said that 80 percent of marriages end in divorce after the death of a child.

"Accosting us like that in public seemed incredibly insensitive, even though he was speaking from his own experience. Alex and I talked over his warning and agreed (or at least *I* thought we agreed) that our marriage was safe from his statistics. After twenty years, we had survived our share of stress, including our daughter's life-threatening illness and several close calls with our business. Once we nearly ran out of cash while we were waiting for one of our customers to pay a disputed bill.

"Because Alex never showed much emotion, I wasn't surprised that he used work to ward off the sorrow of losing our son. I'm not an outwardly emotional person either. Talking was not my outlet as much as writing—poems, short stories, a diary. Mostly I kept my mind actively engaged in work or responsibilities. I couldn't allow myself to dwell on the pain, but gradually I developed some perspective on our loss and its meaning. All the while I thought Alex was having similar conversations with himself, trying to work through the sadness and rebuild our life, but he must have been having an altogether different internal dialogue.

"Just before the accident, we had a disappointing experience with a therapist our son was seeing which, because of the timing, really preyed on us. We thought the family should be included if our son was to gain from therapy, but the therapist flatly refused to talk to us, even on the phone. That left us feeling very shut out. After the accident, the therapist never called us or sent a note. We received one of those printed condolence cards to which he had just signed his name.

"When Alex hired a new assistant, I extended the same home hospitality to her that I did to everyone who came to work for us. The thought of a romance between her and Alex never crossed my mind, not only because of her youth but also because I thought our marriage was secure.

"It's really very hard to reconstruct my mind-set in view of what happened later. Here was a hardworking family man, who valued his reputation in the community, and whose wife was making a major contribution to the business. The last thing you would expect him to do at the age of fifty is to run off to have a baby with a new employee.

"At the time she was hired, my mind was preoccupied with my father's illness. Knowing he had only months to live, I wanted to spend as much time as possible with my mother and him. I was under a lot of strain and expected Alex to give me the kind of emotional support I was in the habit of giving him, but he just busied himself at the office. I was disappointed that he was so disconnected from my distress, because this was the first time I personally needed help from him. Although I felt resentful, I never confronted him.

"Two and a half months after my father died, Alex just walked in from a trip and blurted out that our marriage was over: He wanted a divorce, a baby, and a remarriage, in that order. For consolation, he handed me a round-trip airline ticket to visit my mother.

"I was stunned and horrified. You know, I always believed that a marriage couldn't fall apart unless both parties contributed to the breakup. If a friend had told me that her husband had unilaterally written off their marriage, I would have been certain that she was withholding vital information. Now I know just how innocent and overthrown a spouse can be."

I asked Kathy what Alex had brought up as grievances.

"He mentioned petty annoyances such as I did too many crossword puzzles."

That was a startling echo of Angela's husband. "What bothered him about crossword puzzles?"

"I'm not sure, but I think he was implying that I was doing crossword puzzles when I should have been paying attention to him.

"What really afflicted him, in my opinion, was a desperate need to replace the son we lost. That, of course, was not possible with a postmenopausal wife. While I thought we were having parallel thoughts about our tragedy, he must have been germinating plans to solve his loss in this bizarre way."

With her husband planning to father more dependents, Kathy couldn't afford to delay negotiating a financial settlement.

"Although my mind was in gear enough to know that I had to work quickly to protect our daughter who was nearing college age, my emotions were in shock: I couldn't think or act for myself.

Fortunately, a friend sent me to a capable lawyer, who gave me sound advice and wouldn't let me cave in to Alex's pressure."

Like other victims of rejection, Kathy found that her woes did not end when she and her husband signed the financial settlement paving the way for a divorce.

"There was a period of euphoria when Alex and his girlfriend were really living it up. They went around the world on an extravagant buying trip. Then he moved back into our neighborhood when she became pregnant, as if he wanted everyone to appreciate his young mistress and the evidence that he was about to be an out-of-wedlock father. When the baby was born, he sent announcements to *my* family.

"You would have thought that he would have wanted a divorce as soon as possible so he could legitimize the baby, but he wouldn't pay his financial obligations and, indeed, he refused to accept service of the divorce papers.

"About three years after he left, he called me one December and held a relatively sane conversation about our daughter's plans and his responsibilities. By that time, she was in college. I thought everything would go smoothly after that, but he reneged almost immediately. Not only did he stop paying college tuition, he sent a letter to the registrar stating flatly that she shouldn't be allowed to matriculate if he was expected to pay the bills. I had to sue him.

"Alex kept getting postponements and raising outlandish objections, such as claiming that he had been pressured into signing the settlement agreement. (That was an amazing distortion of facts.)

"When the judge finally ordered Alex to pay, he refused and notified the court that he intended to appeal. He was allowed nine months to 'perfect' his appeal. Since his argument was so flimsy, I thought he would use the appeal threat as an excuse for delay but would not waste money on legal action that had so little chance of success. Exactly nine months to the day, my lawyer called to say that Alex had filed an appeal and that the judge had refused to order him to put up a bond to guarantee payment pending the outcome of the appeal.

"Six months later, the appeals court upheld the original decision on the tuition. But Alex didn't give up: He promptly hired a new lawyer with political connections to attempt to throw out the entire divorce agreement. Finally, three years after the tuition was due, the judge dismissed all of his spurious claims and once again ordered him to pay what he owed.

"Alex complied, but the amount I received was reduced by my hefty legal fees. I don't think I will ever recover from the anxiety of not being able to meet the tuition deadlines and having to dredge and borrow so our daughter wouldn't have to drop out of college. Although she was able to earn money working, she couldn't qualify for aid because of her father's income."

"Did you think he was short of money?"

"Well, I had no way of knowing his financial situation after spending so much money on setting up a new home and the expenses connected with the baby. Legally and morally, he had a contractual obligation to his original family that should have come first."

I wondered how Kathy's daughter interpreted these drastic changes in her father's behavior.

"It's hard for her to remember that Alex was once a good father, a little temperamental but always with the children's welfare at heart. He has been so damaging that I think she is resigned to not having a father anymore. If she marries, there is no chance she will allow herself to be dependent on her husband for economic security."

"When the children were younger, did he favor your son?"

"Not really. He valued achievement, and fortunately both children were achievers. I thought I was married to a man who was a caring father and a decent human being. First there was the betrayal, then the harassment. His answer to the lawsuit was to hook our phone into some kind of computer link so that it would ring intermittently throughout the day and night. I had to remove the extension from the bedroom."

"What do you know about Alex at this time?"

"There have been other visible signs of decline such as hanging around in bars with his wife. It's hard to picture him with a drinking problem since he was only a social drinker when I knew him. Through the business grapevine, I hear that he no longer can be relied on. Alex and reliability used to be synonymous.

"Because I admired his good points, I overlooked many of the difficulties of living with Alex and put my energy and ability into the business with no thought that my "ownership" was contingent on our marriage. I was his dedicated partner for twenty years, and he ended it with the flick of a sentence.

"However," Kathy concluded, "I really try not to dwell on the betrayal. I don't want to be embittered for life."

Other Whispers and Cries

Angela, Diane, and Kathy were all on the receiving end of brutality they couldn't understand, brutality that no one can understand without an education in the psychology of bad-object rage and the interminable vendetta that is its external expression.

Most of the women described moments so dark and events so painful and humiliating that their voices never rose above a whisper.

"The relief of my husband returning home after spending three months with a girlfriend was shattered one week later. We got news that our youngest son died in an automobile accident. My husband, a model father until his affair, showed no emotion whatsoever. All I could discern was this palpable fury at me."

"The weekend after my husband told me he intended to leave, I watched horrified as he lay back in a chair sucking his thumbs and falling fast asleep in a matter of seconds. I phoned the psychiatrist who was treating him but she wouldn't even allow me to describe what I had seen."

"After failing to get the appointment he had coveted, my husband changed abruptly from taking pride in my accomplishments to being acutely jealous. The week before he left, we were guests at a dinner party. I observed him crushing one of our hostess's wine-glasses in his fist. My inner voice told me that his gesture was directed at me."

"Two of our four children picked up and moved across the country, then the worst thing imaginable happened. Our son lost his life in an accident, and our daughter succumbed to anorexia."

"Our younger son grew more and more alienated. After graduating from college, he took a series of jobs in Africa. I didn't see him for *seven* years. That was almost more than I could endure."

"After my husband left, our son turned rebellious and defiant. He got into trouble with the law and twice was placed in juvenile facilities. Now he has a job and is thinking of college, but it was a long nightmare. The pressure on me was brutal—having to support the family financially and emotionally without a cent from my husband—I don't know what saved me from collapse."

*   *   *

Almost every wife described herself as a "basket case" for a long period after the abandonment. Some recalled prolonged periods of depression, weeping, and "shock so severe that I have absolutely no memory of how I got through day to day." A few remembered being very angry and very desperate, and more than a few confided that they were suicidal.

"I had my children to feed, and no money; he had canceled our credit and our health insurance. I thought I would go mad."

"My husband would return frequently to see the children and would be charming to them while treating me like a nanny. That look of indifference, really detestation, just devastated me. A truly caring psychiatrist saved me from committing suicide. My husband paid the bills, but he would not have cared if I had taken my life."

"I was hysterical and finally took my physician's advice and signed myself into a mental hospital for a stay of six weeks."

"I went to the medicine cabinet and swallowed a bottle of my husband's sleeping pills."

"I was in bed for six months with paralyzing back and leg pains that no doctor could diagnose."

"The day he told me he was leaving, I woke up in the middle of the night so livid that I started thrashing him."

"For at least three months, I suffered from such exhaustion that I literally couldn't get out of bed. It was diagnosed as a cardiac problem, but it went away after about six months and has not recurred."

"I was in a continuous state of anger after my husband walked out. My therapist warned me that I was becoming a candidate for a heart attack or a stroke. It took many months, but I did get my wrath under control."

"People kept telling me that I would feel better after I had negotiated a settlement. I dared not tell them that the very thought of such finality touched off the most dreadful churning sensations in my gut. I couldn't picture any future, only suicide when it was over."

*   *   *

After the children, the subject that stirred the most emotion was the adultery. "It wasn't that he went to any great lengths to be discreet; I just wasn't suspicious." Once the affair was revealed, the husbands seemed to aim for maximum humiliation.

"I don't know whether he was looking for approval or publicity, but he seemed to want everybody to know about his affair."

"I had been entertaining my husband's lover for over a year. He had insinuated her into the family as his protégée. She was too young for me to be suspicious, not much older than our children."

"He made no effort to spare my feelings or conceal his philandering. He seemed to take pleasure in showing up at school events arm in arm with his girlfriend."

"Two weeks after he left, he shocked everyone by taking his girlfriend to the annual ball of the charity where he was very well known from having spent years on the board."

"I couldn't believe that he wasn't going to leave me the tickets to our concert series. But no, he immediately took this brand-new girlfriend to sit in the seats we had occupied for twenty years!"

"I thought my husband would have enough shame or sentiment to keep his girlfriend far away from me and the places we occupied together. You can't imagine my shock when I drove out to our country house a few weeks after he left and found that he had been sleeping with her in *our* bed. He made no effort to conceal the evidence."

"While we were attending my mother's funeral, my husband told our teenage son that he was having an affair with his secretary— that was four months before he told me."

"His arrangements with the children seemed calculated to produce unnecessary contact between me and his mistress." (Many wives felt that the children were being exploited to intensify the humiliation.)

"He moved with his girlfriend into an apartment in the same complex, as if he were deliberately trying to torment me."

*   *   *

Atrocious behavior in connection with the adultery is one of the constants in wife rejection. Understanding the syndrome and projective identification sheds a little light. Once revealed, the affair is the ideal antidote to the anxiety. The affair does double service: filling the husband's void and stirring the wife's wrath. The latter, of course, adds visible evidence to confirm the husband's projection that his wife is the one who is angry.

The husband seems to be listening to and acting on a lot of contradictory impulses. One is to exhibit pride in his mistress (his new good object) who has replaced his wife (now his bad object). Another is to stifle his disgust with himself by denigrating his wife (now his scapegoat). Yet another is to sponsor a kind of sinister three-way transaction (triangulation) that involves him, his wife, and his mistress in various forms of interaction.

Here is the magnitude of wife rejection. Every step the rejecter takes to relieve his anxiety seems to have the major side effect of insulting, debasing, and damaging his wife and children. One wife compared her husband to a psychopathic criminal: "He didn't give one whit for his victims."

6

Ostracism and Contempt

▼

This is what can happen to your feelings and your relationships when your husband, whom you loved exclusively, suddenly breaks up the family with a runaway departure, changes his identity by taking on a new partner, and imposes on you a new identity as his enemy.

Your husband absconds and every single thread of your existence comes unraveled. What seemed most reliable in your life is exposed as perishable.

Something shakes loose inside your gut—maybe it's the nerve endings coming unplugged from the sockets in his nervous system where they had made their home for twenty-five years. All you really know is that you feel like a fraction of your former self.

All the structure and redundancy that imparted a sense of security is extinct. Coming home to the empty house fills you with anxiety and dread. Every time you are reminded of your isolation, a drain seems to open and suck out your insides.

Twenty-five years of having a partner with whom to share all of your responsibilities—and then suddenly to be totally on your own.

Up to the moment of that announcement, our children had two parents with a shared outlook and a commitment to be caregivers; suddenly they were confronted with disconnected parents, conflicting agendas, and a family home that no longer contained their family.

Overnight the children who were lovingly prized as "our" children became "my" children. And I no longer controlled the money that had been generously disbursed in their behalf. I recoiled from thinking of them as mine alone and of their father as someone estranged from me, but the facts belied my denial. Arthur was seeing his children occasionally, seeing me rarely, and would not, or could not, entertain the thought of being in the same room with his wife and his children together.

I suspect that our children feel like orphans, but I can only guess because they have gone into hiding. They want nothing to do with what is transpiring between their parents. From their fury and rejection of me, I judge that they will never trust their father, their mother, or anyone else ever again.

Friends vanish at breakneck speed.

You are grateful beyond words to have one indispensable friend who will put her arm around your shoulder when you weep and who even includes you in her family's events. (There may be an inverse ratio between how "nice" your husband was and the rate of disappearance of your friends.) Another friend calls religiously every other week and wants to hear what's happening. She also freely shares her expertise in matrimonial law.

Not one married friend who lives close enough to be useful has volunteered the comfort that I honestly think Arthur (in his normal state) and I would have extended to a close friend who met with such a calamity: "We're here; you can count on us."

Your presence seems to cause genuine consternation. People reverse direction to avoid catching your eye. (Only the babies and the dogs still greet you affectionately.)

You had a busy, active life, your time fully occupied, always more opportunities and invitations than you could juggle. Suddenly your social time is empty. You are alone every evening and every weekend. Nobody says, "Come eat leftovers with us tonight," or "How about joining us for a movie?"

Friends come to town and never call. You telephone them and the greeting is frigid, no mention of getting together. You hear a little hostility, a trace of unfriendliness in someone's voice, and know that the relationship is over. Discussion is futile. Your calls and letters go unanswered.

If you're shy, you find it too lonely and embarrassing to go to social events by yourself. You are so grateful for your part-time job, your indispensable friend, a few luncheon dates, and the movies.

You miss having someone with whom to share ideas, reactions, gossip. Your husband is cutting his monthly checks, leaving you with no money for the activities that used to be mentally and artistically stimulating. You forget appointments, partly out of lethargy and partly for lack of anyone with whom to compare schedules. Every piece of personal mail is a reminder of the gaping vacancy inside.

And you have to be honest about your jealousy. You are very thankful for the few married friends still phoning, and pleased when the wives propose a date for lunch. If only every mention of a family event didn't send a stab of pain through your left ventricle and talk of vacations and intimate dinners shared with a spouse didn't set off reflexes that fill you with mourning. The green-eyed monster burrows at your innards every time you see a husband and wife admiring their children, having fun, being affectionate, exchanging knowing glances.

You also know that another kind of tragedy could have abruptly ended the intimate pleasures of your marriage. But your husband is alive and physically well—and dedicated to depriving you of the substitute comfort of a modicum of financial security.

Only one married friend inquires about your precarious financial condition. The lawyers and accountants who were practically members of your family, whom you had introduced to your husband, are invisible.

The basic message—"You have talents; you can build a life of your own"—does not strike you as particularly uplifting since the unarticulated second part is "Don't ask us for the companionship that will help you recover your self-confidence. In fact, don't call back until you've accomplished your independence on your own."

Someone mumbles about not interfering in a "dispute" between a husband and wife. This seems disingenuous coming from people who are known for speaking out against injustices of all kinds. You dare not inquire why a stronger, less scrupulous husband attacking a weaker, more scrupulous wife does not arouse their social conscience.

When people refuse to talk, there is no way to repair a schism.

Some friends probably found me too willing to confide my personal pain, others may have wanted to retain their good opinion of Arthur, while others may have locked me out as a means of keeping wife rejection from their door, but for a person who was usually available to talk, to listen, and to lend a helping hand, it is an unfathomable insult to be shunned by the people I judged to be my closest friends.

Of the fifty or so people who would have been at the top of the guest list for a twenty-fifth anniversary party—if we had given one—only six or seven are still in my phone book. There has been no word whatsoever from several people with whom I thought I was sharing a lifelong friendship!

Older friendships have revived, newer friends have emerged, but nothing can compensate for the mass defection. (Old college friends are consoling. They call back after you confide that you are in despair, having just retained an attorney to protect you from your husband.)

One of the rejected wives described similar insults. "Sometimes I feel people are deliberately trying to make me feel worse. A friend calls on our anniversary, not to commiserate but to gloat. People simply cut off a phone conversation when they hear my voice without saying I'm busy or I'm sorry or I'll call you back. I am no longer treated as a person entitled to respect."

I asked my companion in rejection whether she had any theories about this tendency to exploit our vulnerability. "Are you familiar with the behavior pattern of wild-pack dogs when one of their number is hurt? They gang up and attack the injured dog until they kill him."

Every memory of the past twenty-five years is curdled by Arthur's betrayal. How can I revise the history of our marriage to account for the present? I believe his glow was once authentic. Exactly when did it turn counterfeit? And why do I still cling to the fantasy that one day his face will light up with joy again when he looks in my direction?

All of the circuits of my life passed through my husband. It was a conscious decision on my part to place marriage and family first. Perhaps I would have been less devastated if I had had a career of my own with separate status and separate income. I would have had some money of my own, responsibilities that would have distracted me from the intensity of my sorrow, and the rudiments for developing an extramarital social network.

On the other hand, I probably would have been more inclined to blame myself for Arthur's rejection. No doubt I would have chided myself for being distracted by professional responsibilities. I probably would have been so self-conscious that I wouldn't have noticed that his grievances had so little to do with the reality of me and so much to do with his fixation on me as the epicenter of seismic shifts inside him.

Last week a friend who knew a little about my study, from having introduced me to a rejected wife, stopped to ask how things were going. When I reported that Arthur was now playing hardball, she tossed her reply over her shoulder, "Well, I guess you expected that, didn't you?"

The answer that she didn't wait to hear was, "No." Despite so many accounts of unscrupulous husbands, I did not think that *my* husband would abuse *me*. I could not conceive of Arthur using financial starvation to enforce his will. If self-respect didn't dictate fair treatment of me, at the very least he would want to preserve his reputation with our children. (I couldn't foresee the degree to which their denial would protect him: They simply won't allow any information that reflects badly on their father through their mental filter.)

After our first couples-therapy session with Betsy, I asked her how Arthur compared with other angry husbands she had encountered in her practice. There was a slight shudder before she answered. "I've seen it when they also turn on the children. I've known them to walk out, lock the door, and never be heard from again."

That's how I learned about my relative good luck. At least *my* husband was angry only at *me*. I was much better off than Angela and many of the wives I was to meet whose husbands rejected the whole family. Arthur is out to demolish me, but thankfully he has maintained a facade of goodwill toward our children and has faithfully paid their college fees.

Knowledge that our children *might* be monitoring his conduct probably deters him from carrying out his threat to sell our house out from under me. After twenty-five years, I had forgotten that he is the owner of this house, the only home our children have known.

I have to count recent changes in property law as another piece of luck. While the spouse whose name is on the deed can sell the house, the proceeds must be divided with the spouse whose name is missing.

Humiliating as it is to be subservient to my husband's whim for a share of the income that used to be mine without question, at least I wasn't left with the burden of supporting dependent children or the necessity of becoming self-supporting after midlife because of a husband who seized all the money and ran.

There have been one or two moments when I think Arthur has sounded a little regretful. Before hanging up on one phone conversation, I asked him what had gone wrong. "I always assumed that we were going to grow old together." His answer conceded some bewilderment. "I guess I thought so, too."

During another phone conversation, he went into overdrive, attacking me for "lying and cheating." When I retorted that he must be confusing me with someone else, because I have a fairly spotless record as far as lying and cheating are concerned, he stopped and was silent for a few seconds. "Yes," he said slowly, "you are an excellent person, Madeline." For just that moment, I think a clear image of *me* may have passed through his head.

He makes no pretense of having found happiness in his new relationship and is not exerting pressure to be legally divorced. His objective is more personal: He wants to rid himself of every reminder that I exist. He bristles when I ask whether he had owed me the elementary courtesy of declaring his dissatisfaction before—instead of after—leaving. That was a mere "oversight," and like everything else, it gets twisted into *my* fault for failing to read his unspoken "misery."

When Arthur refused to resume therapy after the August break (about a year after his announcement), Betsy delivered a discouraging prognosis. She warned me that Arthur would be ruthless in his tactics for keeping me away. That was bad news. I absorbed it while continuing to scan for signs that he might be regaining a measure of feeling for me and for what we had created and built together. I was incapable of taking up arms to wage battle over money.

From my investigation, I now know that many spouses do try to return home after their rage is spent, but alas, Arthur's anger is not diminishing. He continues to wear it like a suit of armor.

That I was going to be treated like a creditor or a business enterprise was established two to three months after his departure. His checks came itemized down to the last penny, as if he were paying an invoice for services or goods. There are no words to describe how it feels to be downgraded from co-owner of your husband's income to an expense item.

Money had never been an issue between us. Neither of us was an impulsive or extravagant spender. My deference to his financial management stemmed from respect for his competence and embarrassment over my ineptitude. Our priorities coincided, whether the decisions involved domestic expenditures, underwriting opportunities for our children, or supporting charitable and civic causes.

During the business crisis, I pressed Arthur to spend less and save more, but retreated when my intervention seemed so unwelcome. He was prudent, but our saving would have been more systematic if he had heeded my advice.

Having experienced what I think should be termed *aggressive abandonment*, and still clinging to a slender hope that Arthur will wake up one morning with his batteries carrying a positive charge for me, I feel entitled to a substantial portion of the income and assets which he earned, but which belonged to all five of us during our marriage. That would be slight enough compensation from my husband for reducing my lifework to rubble.

Within the last two years, there was exactly one occasion when Arthur treated me with courtesy. He took me to lunch, exuded immense charm, and showed some concern for my poor appetite. (Lunches have been occasions for demonstrating to waiters and other diners that the person across the table from him was of no consequence and that breaking up marital property was a topic for casual conversation.)

At this particular lunch, he launched into a sales pitch designed to persuade me to sell our country home (a modest retreat we own together). He didn't claim to need the cash, only that "it would be a good deal for both of us." He dangled his bait: If I would cooperate, we might be able to meet occasionally on a friendly basis and discuss issues pertaining to our children.

In other words, if I would just agree to sell our country house, he would allow me to talk to him about our children. Tempting—he knows that his refusal to co-parent is what is tormenting me the most. However, I have put lots of love and energy into that little house, our children love it also, and my lawyer forbids me to sell any asset without full financial disclosure and a negotiated settlement. Arthur's deal has the markings of doing unto me what others have done unto him, forcing him to sell real estate against his will.

I have developed a personal position on our family homes, which unfortunately has no standing whatsoever in state, federal, or Western law. I feel that all five of us have an implicit title to our homes because our family compact intended them to be shared by Arthur and me and our children and their spouses and offspring. That was the agreement the day before Arthur subtracted himself from the family, and that's the way it should remain according to *my* doctrine of fairness. Matrimonial law is replete with categories of property—premarital, marital, joint, community, equitable distribution—but silent on the subject of children's entitlement to *family* property.

As a weapon of coercion, money is highly efficient. To my knowledge, Arthur's finances have been replenished. Word filters back of expensive travel and gastronomic indulgences. When he wants to force compliance, all he has to do is cut the amount of his monthly check. Sometimes he handles guilt the same way. For example, after giving a Christmas party attended by old friends, which prompted all three children to leave town for the holidays, he slashed the amount of his January check by half. The same occurred when I resisted his pressure to sell our country house.

Whereas financial abuse is specific and leaves a trail that can be documented, emotional abuse leaves an unmarked trail. Money can be demanded in a lawsuit, but not respect. I can't contest his worst offenses: his unbridled contempt for me and his repudiation of our joint commitment to our children.

One fall I phoned to get advice on the furnace and opened with what I thought would be an innocuous question. I asked whether he thought I should arrange to get the furnace cleaned. These were the exact words of his reply: "I took that sh– from you for twenty-five years."

His words pierced like a dart; yet I hadn't the faintest notion of what was behind the outburst. He couldn't have been implying that I had nagged him about household repairs, because on his own initiative he always took charge of maintenance. He loved his basement workshop and insisted on dealing with plumbers and electricians himself. For several months after leaving, he continued to oversee the house. He even promised to pay for a long-overdue paint job and to update the phones. Then all of a sudden, he resigned.

Perhaps my question made him feel guilty or reminded him of how much he missed the house. Perhaps my call coincided with renewed frustration from another source. Whatever the explanation, the venom had its effect.

Without apologizing, he later revised his calendar. He said that the period of his misery had spanned only the "last ten years" of our marriage. Since that matched with the beginning of the decline of the business, it seemed like more than a coincidence of timing, but I knew better than to contribute any interpretations.

The scorn in his voice when he says "you" starts a jackhammer in my stomach. He pronounces the second person singular as if he were speaking to someone whom he detests, a worm or miscreant. I know that contempt for me is a substitute for feeling contempt for himself, but that does not make it any the less insulting. Is it possible that he sounded that hostile before, and I didn't "hear" it? Was there repudiation in the voice that was calling me "darling"?

Arthur seems incapable of keeping a promise. Things disappear from the house when I am away for a weekend: the stereo equipment, furniture, paintings, and, of course, his huge collection of tools. Even after he *pledged* never again to use his key (to which he is entitled by law) without notifying me in advance, he removed valuables while I was away for several weeks caring for my parents. My heart sinks when I come home to an empty space where a cherished possession used to sit, but I don't call the police. I know that my husband was the thief.

In the presence of a new therapist, Arthur agreed to spend two years working out our relationship with each other and with our children before negotiating a financial settlement. The very next month, he cut the amount of his check again, notifying me that I would have to retain a lawyer instead of a therapist for protection.

The words that have the most hurting power are those having to do with our children. He fires them at me like bullets: "We are not a family anymore. . . . Our children are adults. . . . They don't need us. . . . They can take care of themselves."

"But our *children's* problems will always be *our* problems." He doesn't answer. This indifference must have something to do with his emotional fragility because it is such a changeover from the father who paid attention to every up and down in the lives of his children.

Although Arthur has been financially responsible toward his/our children, he has not been generous. When he accused me of "seething with anger" three years ago, it was pure projection, because I was foolishly optimistic that his affair would be temporary. Now alternating currents of pain and anger do surge inside me. I am powerless to influence the way our children are being treated either emotionally or financially. Until they are established themselves, Arthur will be able to claim all of the prerogatives that go with being the parent who is the source of loans and gifts.

The worst offense to me and the person Arthur knew me to be is the snatching away of our children's heritage: not only the homes and possessions that should have passed on to them, but the legacy of belonging to a family that loves and cares for one another, that does not injure or betray. That is the kind of family I thought our children had acquired as their birthright. It was a heritage that came from my parents, and it is not within my power to hand it on to our children.

An incident last year, which deprived Arthur of the protective cover of invisibility, interrupted our children's denial. No one overhears those wholesale condemnations on the phone; only anonymous bystanders eavesdrop as he callously disposes of the touchstones of my life in a restaurant; and I am the only one who reads the insults that arrive inside an envelope. For three years he managed never to be in the same room with me and our children. All of a sudden there was no escape. Parental responsibilities brought us together in the outpatient surgical department of a local hospital to wait out a procedure on our son.

Our older daughter walked in on a revealing scene. I was sitting next to the only vacant chair in the waiting room, and Arthur was standing beside me. That he wouldn't sit next to me and wouldn't join us for coffee was not lost on her. For a while, I thought he would never speak directly to me, but after three hours, he finally took a chair at right angles to mine. A few minutes later, conversation turned to Shakespeare, and he looked me in the eye and recalled a production of *Much Ado About Nothing* we had seen together. When it was time for lunch, he went out and bought sandwiches for the three of us.

Then the surgeon appeared, and we crowded together to get his news. He was honest enough to admit that the expensive surgery was unnecessary: He had not found the condition he suspected. For me it was confirmation of the mistakes that occur when parents are divided. I had counseled waiting to see whether the symptoms recurred but was taken out of the loop because of Arthur's uncritical endorsement of our son's impatience.

The deep freeze made enough of an impression on our daughter that she advised her father not to attend a forthcoming family wedding because it would make "everybody too uncomfortable." This was the *first* time that Arthur had been asked to give up anything. The day after he told the bride of his decision not to come, I received another letter threatening to sell our house in the city, the one in his name, and the check that arrived the following week was cut in half.

It would be unrealistic for me to anticipate that Arthur will recover from his "allergy" in the foreseeable future, but for all our sakes, I still hope that he will one day shake off the tyranny of his malignant anger.

Looking at the hurt and damage of rejection through the eyes of twenty-five other women who did not judge their marriages to be precarious and whose feelings for their husbands were at least admiring, if not passionate, I can't escape the deduction that these bonding crises must also snuff out marriages that were already troubled and that families must suffer much worse repercussions when a spouse or parent who has always been surly or punishing or unprincipled deteriorates into bad-object rage.

You may wonder what could be worse, but there are husbands who more or less leave their wives and children for dead. It is fair to say that the more menacing, dangerous, or practiced they are at abuse and deprivation, the less likely it is that the legal system will intervene to protect the family.

To the question of whether all of the victims of bad-object rage are as pleasing and honorable as the group whom I interviewed, I would answer that it is hard to imagine rejection happening to a wife whose temperament was habitually selfish and antagonistic, because she wouldn't be patient during the early period of hostility and withdrawal.

Could a husband's bonding crisis be triggered by actions of his wife instead of extramarital pressures? Certainly. A wife might knowingly or accidentally tip her husband's tolerance by directing strong criticism, or challenging his control, or asking for emotional support that he can't give. She might also set off a crisis by pressuring him to earn more money or by getting involved with another man. A bonding crisis could also be a reaction to onerous *family* burdens, such as chronic illness.

Nothing rules out the possibility of one spouse's rejection triggering a reactive crisis in the partner. Returning the anger and punishment in kind was not in the behavioral repertoire of the women I interviewed, but it must be a common occurrence.

On the other hand, it would be a mistake to charge all sudden exits to the syndrome. If the departing spouse is self-conscious about his or her actions and willing to deal fairly with the spouse left behind, then the leave-taking does not fit either wife rejection or *aggressive* abandonment.

Once we understand the dynamics of a bonding crisis as it infects

131

one spouse's thoughts and feelings, it dawns on us that bad-object rage (like projections) can be an interloper in other relationships besides marriage. One party's prolonged, projected, incurable anger can become the active ingredient in relationships between parent and child, child and parent, mentor and protégé, supervisor and subordinate, as well as between partners, colleagues, and friends. It's conceivable that bad-object feelings are phantoms that dwell in the collective unconscious of many relationships.

Because I persisted in trying to see and talk to my husband, I saw more evidence of visible rage than most rejected wives would be likely to observe. It would be more common for a rejecting husband to maintain physical distance and dispense abuse and harassment via telephone, lawyers, and the postal service. If a husband doesn't see his wife too often or for too long, he may be able to keep his facial mask in place. Inserting a third party may serve to buffer the anxiety of meeting one on one.

Older children realized that they were being manipulated to be present as bystanders when a face-to-face encounter between parents was about to take place. Some of the fathers dropped the bombshell about the affair or the intention to divorce first on the child, as if the child should be the messenger to deliver the news to Mother.

There was nothing temporary or superficial about the wounds suffered by the children of rejected mothers in the group interviewed. Mothers reported shock, depression, defiance, school dropouts, smoldering resentment, arrested development, and, regardless of age, distrust and anger.

In most of the families, the children were strongly attached to their father before the sudden abandonment. In the first year, several of the mothers had to suffer in silence insults along the lines of: "Dad is doing a lot better adjusting to the change than you are." The mothers took the blaming as an indication that their children were in an emotional state in which it felt safer to criticize Mother than to surrender their high opinion of Father.

It is doubtful that children who loved and admired their parents will ever be able to understand or accommodate the abandonment of one by the other. The effect of such blatant betrayal within the family is to lose confidence in all relationships.

Even when fathers appeared to remain faithful to their children, the inconsistency of being ingratiating with offspring and malicious toward their mother was not lost on the children. And so many of the rejecting husbands merged the children with bad objects to be repudiated along with the wife. What can children do with the shock of being excised, neglected, and/or damaged by their father, particularly a father who had lighted up their youth with affection and an appetite for life?

Judith Wallerstein, among others, has punctured our complacency about divorce. Not only did she find divorce more than a temporary dislocation in the lives of the sixty families in her study, she also found a "sleeper effect" among children: defiance, depression, and distrust developing and persisting ten and fifteen years after the divorce. Since the group selected for her study were judged to be on the higher end of the scale of responsibility, the proportion of fathers rejecting their children both emotionally and financially came as a shock. Not one father, wealthy or not, paid his children's college tuition.

The son of one of the mothers I interviewed, a college junior, gave voice to his resentment when he had to scramble to get a loan approved after his father reneged on a lifelong pledge to pay tuition. "It would be better if my father were dead. Then I could remember him for the past and forget these last years when he stopped being my father and became my enemy."

The results of Barbara Cain's interviews with college-age students whose parents had recently divorced also contradict the conventional wisdom that young adults are able to take parental divorce in stride.

Cain, a psychologist at the University of Michigan, concludes that parental divorce for young adults is "a disruptive, wrenching and in many instances a disillusioning experience. . . . Bereft of parents as moral exemplars, these youngsters adopt reactive strategies that range from defiant self-indulgence to abstemious pleasure-avoidant behavior."

Of the forty-eight students she interviewed, Cain noted that fully half believed their parents' marriage to be ideal and their family life to be exemplary. The tendency, of course, is to assume that the students didn't know the whole story. However, if the divorce started with one parent departing suddenly in the mode of wife rejection, then the abandoned parent may have been caught as completely off guard as the child.

For some of the students, the pain of losing the family history and family home was almost unbearable. One young man told of sitting on the floor and weeping while the furniture was being moved out of his childhood home.

Every observer of the divorce scene seems to pose the same question: Why can't parents set aside their warfare to protect the children? I would suggest that attitudes toward children and accommodation to former spouses vary with the degree to which rational decision-making informs the divorce. Since divorces stemming from the rejection syndrome are necessarily marked by a one-sided vendetta, you are asking the impossible if you want the aggressive mate to control his rage and the nearly impossible if you expect the innocent mate to turn the other cheek.

I hope that this evidence of wife rejection as a sequence and a nightmare is sufficient to convince readers that prevention and protection—the subject I will turn to next—ought to be high on the agenda of all individuals and groups who feel that marriage is better than divorce and that what can be learned about the causes of marital breakdown can be used to promote marital longevity.

7

Warnings and Advisories
from Hindsight

▼

My mother once explained some rules of her generation that absolutely flabbergasted me. They related to a virtual ban on second marriage for a widow while her daughter was still single. According to my mother, it was incumbent on her sister (my aunt) to refuse several proposals of marriage in the years following her husband's death because it would have been "improper" for her to remarry before her daughter had found a husband.

This outdated social prohibition comes to mind because it reflects the kind of fatalism that I have encountered in relation to wife rejection. Somehow, this too is the kind of insult that the loser is supposed to swallow without complaint. An abandoned wife is allowed to regain her standing by remarrying but otherwise must accept secondary status as if it had been ordained by higher authorities.

A code requiring a widow to sacrifice her marital opportunities for her daughter seems antiquated. Yet a code that is not too dissimilar has played a part in keeping wife rejection a closely held secret. A rejected wife tends to comply with the pressure from friends and therapists not to fuss too loudly about her husband's betrayal—this is what is called "ladylike" behavior.

Of course, this ladylike compliance is what positioned her for rejection in the first place. She was patient and nonconfrontational toward her husband when he began manipulating her to receive his destructive projections. All of the wives interpreted their husbands' evasion and ill temper as symptoms of distress, never suspecting that the stage was being set for rejection.

What follows is a first attempt to compile the warning signs of a bonding crisis, the telltale changes in behavior that might alert a wife to the possibility that her husband is incubating bad-object delusions with her playing the part of bad object.

Some event—an injury, insult, setback, or sadness—overloads his emotional circuits. He wants to bury his conflicts and can't be persuaded to talk about "what's bothering him." These are some of the outward personality changes that the wives whom I interviewed observed but misinterpreted or overlooked:

Hostility.   Outbursts of temper or a prolonged state of bad temper. Indifference to your welfare. Blaming you for mishaps that would never have been blamed on you before (projection). Seems to be deliberately frustrating you, yet doesn't "understand" what you are talking about when you complain (passive aggression). Sets up situations calculated to incite you to anger (projective identification).

Withdrawal.   Less affection, less sex. Change of habits: spending less time with you, asking less help from you, going out evenings when he has never done that before, avoiding you as if he were having an allergic reaction to being in your presence (Chernobyl effect).

Personality change.   Change in attitudes and interests. New group of friends. Rejuvenation activities (fitness, jogging, adolescent pursuits), impulsivity, euphoria, less tolerance for postponing gratification. Particularly ominous when he claims to be unaware of any change (denial, compartmentalization, false euphoria, regression).

Secret pastimes.   Usually adultery but could be other activities that take him out of the home and are inconsistent with previous business or leisure activities. New set of companions of either sex.

Lack of self-awareness.   Not able to accept criticism or to criticize himself. Literally unaware of hurting or neglecting you as if it either had not happened or were happening to someone else (compartmentalization, denial, dissociation).

Emotional shallowness. Feelings are bland. "Out to lunch." Juvenile quality in needing to have his way. Unwilling or unable to react to serious problems. Disconnected thinking (dissociation).

Withholding cooperation. Won't participate in decision-making. Won't make a decision himself; won't let you make one either. Seems to be doing opposite of what will please you; denies your allegations when you complain but persists nevertheless. Unyielding. Unwilling or unable to change his mind on the basis of evidence (passive aggression, compartmentalization).

Sudden projections. False assumptions about your attitudes or thinking. Accusations that have no basis in fact. More serious when he seems to confuse you with someone—a parent or a rival, for example—who has harmed him (making you into the bad object). Super-serious when he has premonitions that you or someone else is suicidal.

It can be misleading to classify quarrels and disagreements according to specific issues, thereby missing the source of conflict, which may lodge in a generalized need to control in areas where he feels threatened. Conversations that don't make a lot of sense should not be dismissed. It would be useful to record dissonant remarks so that you can try to discern a pattern.

Based more on hearsay than the experience of the women I interviewed, I would also place a warning label on lavish parties honoring a wife's birthday or the couple's anniversary. I have heard enough reports of a husband walking out after throwing a big party—ostensibly for his wife, perhaps for himself—to warrant caution when a party seems more exhibitionistic than sincere.

I hope that information also will emerge on the internal thought processes. What are they *thinking* when they start leading a life that is so discordant with their previous standards? When I was three or four, I remember cutting the feathers off my mother's hat and thinking that she would not notice the damage if I swept up all the clippings. Is reality testing reduced to that of a preschooler? What has happened to self-monitoring, to what psychologists call the "observing ego"? Do they think that no one will notice the incongruities in their behavior? (In truth, this ostrichlike assumption works in their favor. People choose not to notice.)

This is a tentative list and a first try in an undertaking that needs collaboration. It attempts to cover the visible changes that should be interpreted as warning signals of marital drift. As more information is contributed, more of the picture will develop.

Perhaps publicity about the syndrome will prompt husbands or wives to share their experiences of a close call with rejection. What happened to intercept the chain reaction? Why did the good-object glue hold? Are there lessons for other couples?

It is the *pattern*, not an isolated episode of withdrawal, that is worrisome. If you sense that your husband (or wife) is strangely ill at ease in your presence and unaware of being inconsiderate or hurtful to you, an alarm ought to go off. Better to worry and take corrective measures than deny and discover your blindness after he (or she) announces a bonding crisis.

What to do? Most important: *Get to work while the good-object glue is holding.*

I remember a Sunday late in the business strife when we were working together in the kitchen and Arthur criticized me excessively three times in rapid succession. I borrowed one of our children's expressions to notify him that he was displacing irritation on me: "I feel as if you are getting on my case." He instantly became more congenial.

Although I didn't know it at the time, telling someone how their behavior is making you feel is one of the more effective ways of gaining attention. You send your message without sounding accusatory and without making the other person feel guilty.

But that wasn't my general practice when something offended me. I often used less constructive methods—such as appeasement, withdrawal, or retaliation—which do nothing to improve communication.

Appeasement was my response to the stress during the business crisis. I extended myself to keep the peace, soothe tensions, and make our homelife as agreeable as possible. Being available to absorb some of the strain seemed like a small contribution from the partner who was allowed to sit on the sidelines while her husband took the brunt of negotiations that were as demanding as they were debilitating. At the time, it seemed only fair to put aside my preferences and accommodate to his.

I think that most of the women were conditioned to placate their husbands when they were under stress. However, the results would probably have been the same if we had responded with withdrawal or retaliation. If a wife retreats into silence, or spins off to do her own thing, or returns the hostility in kind, communication will surely come to a halt. Her husband won't tell her how bad he is feeling until he is in the panic of a bonding crisis, at which point he will be in tears or fury or ecstasy as he announces that he intends to stay afloat by jettisoning his wife.

There are crucial differences between getting angry and expressing hurt, also between criticizing someone's actions and telling that person what effect their actions are having on you. When you lose your temper, your recipient feels entitled to reciprocate in kind, even if you happen to be wholly right and he or she happens to be wholly wrong. Fending off with a shield of silence has the same effect of ruling out discussion so there will be no discovery of what is disrupting your relationship. By the same token, criticism delivered in the form of an accusation or attack seems to justify withdrawal or retaliation, neither of which is conducive to communication.

Becoming shock absorbers instead of critics of their husbands came naturally to many of the wives, who told of performing previous duty as shock absorbers for their parents. In my case, I think that it was my extended service as shock absorber for our children that prepared me for appeasing Arthur during the crisis. So many satisfactions flowed from motherhood that I overlooked our children's penchant for trampling on me in private, though not when Arthur was around to insist on respect for both of us.

It didn't seem too abnormal for children to unleash some (it seemed like all) of their frustrations on Mommy. Since they were

139

growing up well in other respects, I conceded this overuse of displacement as the price of their passage into adulthood. Like a lot of mothers of my generation, I aimed for a caring relationship based on mutual respect without threats or guilt trips.

Until Arthur's bonding crisis, I would have described our children as "emotionally privileged." They had parents who gave them unqualified love and encouragement, teachers who admired their accomplishments, and friends who made them feel appreciated among peers. Their need to hook me into their waste-disposal system seemed to exceed my will to extract myself.

It goes without saying that I am no longer so indulgent when someone storms at me in order to shake off an insult that originated elsewhere. It is only human to dispose occasionally of irritation on an innocent party, but at the very least, we ought to apologize afterward. Failure to retract or apologize looks suspiciously like *unconscious* displacement—when you don't even know that you are taking out your frustration on a convenient bystander. Kissing and making up after an altercation leaves out the crucial debriefing step: You never know whether the other party is merely regretting the strife or is actually taking responsibility for his or her contribution to it.

Our family succumbed to the demon that convinced my husband that his wife was his enemy. This demon, of course, does not confine its intrusions to husband-wife relationships. It can spread like a contagion through a family. For every wife who reported children clustering during the crisis of abandonment, there was another who had the topsy-turvy experience of being the target of blistering attacks from the children. "You would have thought I was the parent who had deserted the family."

From the mothers' point of view at least, it seemed that a disproportionate number of the children, having been so deeply hurt by their fathers, took out their frustration on their mothers. Mothers are blamed for the drop in their standard of living, for the father's hostility, for the bad grades in school, for being too nice, too demanding, too stingy, too generous, et cetera, et cetera.

What do you do when somebody you care about is incurably mad at you? When appeasement, withdrawal, and self-defense are useless? The methods of "active listening" recommended by Betsy, the therapist who finally shed some light on rejection, apply to rejecting children as well as spouses. Her instructions emphasized the "don'ts." "Do not interpret, insult, accuse, or lay a guilt trip. Do not use diagnostic terms like denial, projection, narcissism, or passive aggression, which suggest you have superior understanding of their behavior. What you must remember is that people who have run out of self-esteem cannot tolerate guilt, nor do they have the emotional resilience to experience guilt or to learn from mistakes."

When a spouse seems to be withdrawing, "safe" responses are those that don't close down communication. It's safe to reflect back the emotion, restate the content of the interaction, or explain the impact the behavior is having on the recipient: "You sounded so angry at me just now: I don't understand what I did." "I feel as if the unspoken rules of our marriage have suddenly changed." "I feel as if I am always being put on the defensive." "It may be my imagination, but I have the impression that we are spending less of our free time together." "I wonder if you realize how much my feelings were hurt by what you just said."

The above advice applies to exchanges with anybody who is too irrational to listen to reason. When they put on their armor, they will lash out at you if you try to puncture it. They are too fragile for direct confrontation.

Another helpful intercession is to name the feeling that you are observing in the other person. "You seem angry" [irritated, distressed, et cetera] is a very useful intervention. The person may be experiencing inchoate, diffuse anxiety and may not be in touch with the anger, sadness, or depression. Labeling the emotion may give relief and may also open the way to some heartfelt conversation.

A mistake I made frequently was trying to talk someone out of feelings that seemed inappropriate. Active listening counsels you to accept as valid whatever feeling a person expresses. Help comes in the form of a safe-conduct to express feelings, not in glossing over or distracting from feelings that seem misplaced.

You also have to be honest with yourself. Are you failing to ask exploratory questions because you are afraid of discovering how deeply troubled your spouse is? I have to ask myself whether one of the reasons I took Arthur at his word—that he was holding up under the pressure—was because I would have been quite lost and scared if I had known that he was crumbling inside.

Once, a few months before his announcement, Arthur did say, in an almost offhand way, that he felt like a failure. My heart ached, but I answered with a pep talk on his accomplishments instead of a simple invitation to tell me more. When I bungled that opportunity, I was still looking forward to the vacation that would be a relaxed setting "to let it all hang out."

This is the bare bones of an "active listening guide" to what to avoid and what to try when you want to reach someone who is not responding to reason. The advice derives from the work of Carl Rogers, the influential psychologist who devised nondirective interviewing to help patients recover their authentic feelings, and Tom Gordon, who refined and popularized noninvasive techniques for improving family communications in *Parent Effectiveness Training*. The methods take into account what seems to be universal in human nature: our reluctance to reveal ourselves unless we feel validated and safe from shame and attack.

There is another possibility that has to be faced. What if the undivulged secret turns out to be an affair? If you have been faithful and are in love with your spouse, how can you feel anything but insult and searing betrayal? The lesson of wife rejection, however, is that the extramarital affairs often function as alternative forms of stress management.

The broader lesson is that affairs serve unconscious needs. Herbert Strean has written about patterns in extramarital affairs. It appears that only a minority of affairs involve pairing with a more fulfilling, more compatible mate.

Marion Solomon agrees that affairs are not causes of the breakup of a marriage but are symptoms of underlying problems or attempts to deny such problems. "An affair may function as a distance regulator, as an instrument of revenge, as the expression of a need for an affirming other, as a way to convince oneself of one's attractiveness, sexual potency or lovableness."

The womanizer who continually needs an extramarital sexual fix or conquest is in a different category from the husband who is incubating the anxiety of a once-in-a-lifetime bonding crisis. If the affair comes to light early enough, it might be interpreted less as a repudiation of the wife than as an escape from a dilemma, more of a storm warning to be heeded than an offense to be met with withdrawal and recriminations.

What if your self-help measures fail? Suppose you have done your best to free your husband to talk about those private feelings of fear, despair, insecurity, jealousy that wake us up in the middle of the night, and he still maintains his silence or makes hollow declarations to the effect that "something must be wrong with you because nothing's wrong with me" (notice the projection). Then it's time to scout for a therapist with a sympathetic personality and a profound understanding of projections and object relations.

In the interim, a self-help group like Adult Children of Alcoholics (ACOA), an offshoot of Alcoholics Anonymous, might provide a setting for reflection and self-discovery. Although intended for the comfort and growth of children of alcoholics, ACOA can be useful for anybody who grew up in a dysfunctional household. These are self-perpetuating groups whose meetings can be attended for the purpose of sitting quietly without speaking or for being recognized to share personal suffering with a circle of people who will listen respectfully and sympathetically.

The nationwide network of telephone listening and referral services called CONTACT, or other crisis hotlines, might be an option if your husband would consider talking about his problems on the phone with a volunteer who is trained in active listening and pledged to confidentiality.

At the point of seeking a therapist, you should also be taking self-protective measures like educating yourself about the sources of the family income and stockpiling some savings in your name. This advice comes directly from Marie, whose husband tricked her into signing papers that put their joint stock account in his name only, embezzlement that occurred not because she lacked financial acumen but because he was the investor and she trusted him implicitly.

Of course, this is the advice that has been issuing from the women's movement for some time. It's very sound, but I hope it doesn't translate into an attitude that you have only yourself to blame if you are betrayed and have not earned or sequestered funds of your own. There are many, many circumstances—illness and disability being just two examples—which may prevent either spouse from working. Aren't we cheating our marriages and our families if we continue to subscribe to a divorce code that doesn't value anything but the monetary contribution to marriage?

Excluding marriages that end out of necessity as a result of cruelty, dishonesty, or divergent life-styles, we know that many other marriages break up unnecessarily when one partner reaches an emotional impasse, wife rejection being an extreme example. Whether a motivated spouse can succeed in preventing the unnecessary divorce depends to a great extent on the resources made available by the community. Help with health care, child care, job protection, and alcohol and drug treatment are some of the obvious contributions government and private programs can make to saving endangered marriages. Any initiative that works to lighten adversity or preserve self-esteem should be regarded as an inoculation against divorce.

As for rejected wives or wives on the verge of being rejected, like all victims of false charges they need an intermediary—in fact, two intermediaries: a caring, informed therapist and a divorce code that values families. I will try to explore some of the weaknesses and possibilities for these intermediaries to give their best effort to saving marriages and protecting the innocent in divorce.

8

Headhunting for a Therapist

▼

After so many personal disappointments with therapists, it may seem naïve of me to continue to propose that therapy can help save marriages when stress triggers the self-protective mechanisms that lead to scapegoating and rejection. My confidence can't really be put to the test until enough therapists acknowledge the existence of the syndrome and place it on their professional agendas.

Fatalism seems to be the prevailing attitude among therapists who know about bad-object rage and its catastrophic consequences for a family. They treat it as a caveat emptor situation for the wife and children. "I'll take care of your husband. You'll have to watch out for yourself."

Having spent my working and volunteer time among educators, social workers, and health-care professionals, I find it incongruous that members of any helping profession would wave off a family at risk for such life-destroying abuse. Of course, this criticism applies only to therapists who know enough about projections to wonder whether a husband is reconstructing his wife as his bad object when he suddenly needs to discard her. Therapists who themselves do not grasp the magnitude of the danger could not possibly warn a potential victim.

I wish I could cite one approach to therapy as the most promising for helping a marriage survive a spouse's bonding crisis, but so long as secrecy prevails about the wife-rejection syndrome, there will be no incentive to synthesize an approach to intervention.

These recommendations regarding what qualities to look for and what to avoid in a therapist have evolved from four years of trial and error during which I have discussed the specifics of my problem and the general outlines of wife rejection with at least two hundred therapists. I have also learned a great deal about the possibilities and limits of therapy from attending numerous courses and workshops at psychoanalytic and psychiatric institutes and Family Therapy training centers. My investigation has been confined to conventional therapy in the sense of a course of treatment or counseling that takes place in an office and involves engaging the patients or clients in talking about their problems.

One conclusion that seems inescapable is that it is virtually impossible for a neophyte to make an informed choice among the mind-boggling variety of therapies and therapists. You really have to be in the field to be able to read the menu and know what questions to ask. Furthermore, needing a therapist implies not being at your emotional best and therefore not at your sharpest for making judgments about people.

A lot of former therapy patients will tell you how lucky they were to find the right therapist in their moment of dire need. "I was desperate." "I was a mess." "I was in a fury." "I was coming apart at the seams." "I may seem composed and successful now, but you wouldn't have thought so if you had seen me three years ago." Many patients are so taken with the insights and skill of their therapists that they decide to go into the field themselves.

Because medical specialists and accreditations are publicized and regulated, the search for a medical doctor to treat a rare disorder can be conducted in a more orderly fashion than the quest for a therapist with a particular background and skills. When you need a medical doctor for a difficult problem, you don't hesitate to burn up the wires to get referrals. Publicity is exactly what you want to avoid when you are frantically looking for a therapist with whom you can discuss your premonitions that your husband is brewing a bonding crisis.

Whatever your preconceptions about therapy or therapists, there is really no way to circumvent the need for a mental-health specialist to treat a mental-health problem. Your heart may be breaking but a cardiologist can't prescribe for it.

Advisory No. 1. If you have observed a number of the warning signs of wife rejection, assume there's a marital problem even though your spouse hasn't specifically notified you that he's unhappy.

Advisory No. 2. Don't urge your husband to see a therapist by himself. He could become wedded to somebody who is either unskilled or indifferent to marriages and families.

Advisory No. 3. Look for a therapist who has had extensive experience working with couples but get to know him or her before you invite your husband to attend a session. Once you are both involved, it is very hard to change therapists should you become dissatisfied with the quality of help. (This also applies to screening therapists to work with your children or with the whole family together.)

Advisory No. 4. Don't confine your search to therapists who advertise themselves as family or couples therapists. You want a therapist who has worked with individuals enough to understand unconscious defenses and is also skilled and experienced at working with couples.

Advisory No. 5. Ask all the questions that occur to you about education, philosophy, affiliations, methods, biases, and experience. Look at the bookshelf for clues.

Does the therapist think in terms of object relations, psychodynamics, projective identification, and/or systems and collusions? Will more attention be paid to the systems that have developed within the family for processing conflict or to gaining insight into the emotional insecurities and unconscious defenses that burden the relationship between husband and wife?

I like to ask whether the therapist has a formal arrangement for consulting with colleagues or a supervisor on difficult problems. Assuming confidentiality is preserved, I find the existence of backup support reassuring.

Advisory No. 6. Look for a therapist who is authentically warm and capable of creating a tranquil environment where you and your husband will feel safe confiding your secrets. Look also for an activist outlook toward helping, since patience and perseverance may be needed to enlist your husband's cooperation.

Advisory No. 7. Excuse yourself politely if a prospective therapist says that he or she will be glad to treat you individually, but that confidentiality rules out seeing a couple or a family together.

Advisory No. 8. If your husband has already gone over the edge and announced a bonding crisis, you ought to be able to tell from the therapist's expression whether he or she is aware that something dire has happened.

Advisory No. 9. Beware of a therapist who insists that your husband couldn't be so angry at you unless you had done something to provoke it. The therapist may not understand projections or narcissistic rage.

Advisory No. 10. Don't sit still if the therapist seems to be stirring up animosity. One woman said that the therapist opened the first session by turning to her husband and asking, "What do you hate about your wife?" Later in the same session the therapist seemed to put words in her husband's mouth: "Maybe you never loved your wife."

Advisory No. 11. Don't settle for a therapist whose philosophy is incompatible with yours. If you believe that change comes through introspection and self-examination, and the therapist belittles talk of emotions or unconscious defenses, then you probably are not well suited to one another.

The same applies if you sense that the therapist does not fully share your convictions about the tragic consequences of ill-considered divorce.

Advisory No. 12. Don't be overly impressed by celebrity status. Some therapists who have made their reputations by writing or personal appearances are better writers or lecturers than they are clinicians. You want someone who will be dedicated to helping you and who is more interested in people than theories.

Philosophy, personality, and training should all be considered. It may be necessary to interview a number of candidates before selecting one.

Therapists are practiced at looking you in the eye and nodding as though they agree with you. The only way to find out whether they are nodding agreement, or merely encouraging you to talk, is to keep asking questions and evaluating their answers.

You may feel that you can't afford to pay for too many sampling sessions, but you will be even less happy about wasting time and money on a therapist who turns out to be unskilled or unsympathetic with your problem.

Introducing a therapist into a stressful situation is a way to relieve some of the tension. One of the functions of a therapist, according to psychoanalyst Donald Winnicott, is to serve as a "container," a surrogate to hold a patient's anxiety until healing occurs. At the same time, the therapist gains enormous sway over the patient's attitudes. The epithet "shrink" betokens our awareness of the therapist's power to influence our thoughts and actions.

A prospective patient or client is apt to pay too much attention to the therapist's advertised clientele, such as families or couples, and too little to the significant variations in philosophy and clinical methods.

Family Therapy, for example, should be understood as *one* method for conducting therapy and not as *the* method of choice for family problems. It's different with couples therapy. Couples are the clientele but the methods vary.

Couples therapy that is based on Family Therapy methods usually involves discussion and dissection of interpersonal behavior, how we use and misuse one another, and how we repeat patterns and themes that pervade our families of origin.

Marital therapy that is influenced by psychoanalytic thinking will focus more on the intrapsychic or internal struggles of the individuals as they affect the relationship. These therapists will encourage the couple to explore their feelings and emotions, the unconscious transmissions that pass between them, and the way each spouse fits the other into his or her pattern of object relations.

The reason I have been capitalizing Family Therapy is to draw a distinction between an approach to therapy that goes by that name and therapy for families. Family Therapy is a school of therapy that is conducted according to a set of guidelines that have been evolving in the last thirty years. The emphasis is on the here and now—the interpersonal exchange—what family members say and do as they discuss their problems and the patterns and themes that recur from one generation to the next. Family Therapists (sometimes more than one is present) are active observers and managers of the sessions. They try to investigate and clarify the sources of conflict and devise interventions to help the family system function with less friction.

Some of the names that are prominent in Family Therapy include: Minuchin, Ackerman, Haley, Bowen, Boszormenyi-Nagy, and Selvini Palazzoli (of Milan, Italy).

Family Therapists have introduced many innovative methods for learning about and modifying family behavior. Thanks to genotyping or family mapping, videotaping, and procedures that encourage collaboration among therapists, they have been able to make many astute observations about the patterns or "systems" that bind a family. Their expertise is in interpersonal behavior patterns: what family members say, how they act, the entrenched alliances, rivalries, and scapegoating that develop among and between parents, children, and spouses.

All theories of therapy that hold that insight is a prerequisite for change owe a debt to Sigmund Freud's exploration of the unconscious, which ranks as one of the seminal "discoveries" of the twentieth century. Because Freud was prolific in his writings and fairly intolerant of dissenting opinions, it is easy to quarrel with specific pronouncements. But every time we are aware of being captive of emotion over reason, we have to credit his invention of "analysis" for providing the diagnostic tool that enables us to study our unconscious motivations and defenses, the parts of us that cannot be imaged on X rays or scans.

Many of Freud's descendants still confine themselves to individual therapy, eschewing group, couples, and family work. They practice traditional psychoanalysis, which commits a therapist and patient to working together at a slow pace over a long period of time to understand and overcome the unconscious obstacles that keep the patient from realizing his or her potential.

Some psychoanalysts have developed briefer forms of treatment for individuals who haven't the time, funds, or inclination to spend five or so years probing dreams, unconscious associations, and projections to work problems through to some core understanding of what Freud called "making the unconscious conscious." Other analysts have devised ways of working with groups, couples, and families that incorporate both insights from psychoanalysis and techniques from Family Therapy.

My talks with so many providers and consumers of therapy has inspired respect for open-ended treatment. Some therapists make claims for flamboyant, one-shot cures. No doubt some people are helped by a stroke of brilliant intervention. In general it seems that psychological problems have to be worked through slowly. There is nothing equivalent to an antibiotic to eradicate infections that invade our self-esteem. Getting to know our inner selves and gaining control over our behavior appear to be labor-intensive activities.

Therapy for a couple on the brink of wife rejection is a challenging assignment, but that is exactly what conscientious therapists are always accepting. They are accustomed to treating patients who are in emotional *extremis*, either from internal stresses or from exceptional pressures from their environment.

In order to be accredited, therapists usually have to undergo a significant regimen of therapy themselves. The methods they practice on their patients inevitably emulate the methods that were practiced on them. To gain credentials as a psychoanalyst, a therapist has to spend many years in personal analysis and then more years in a training analysis and supervision by a senior analyst.

Mental health as a whole might change for the better if a decision to seek therapy were regarded as a sign of strength instead of weakness. The person who takes the first step in admitting that something is wrong is more enlightened and courageous than the person who clings to some transparent excuse such as "Therapy is a fraud" or "I don't believe in therapy" or "Therapy might inhibit my creativity" or "I don't know anybody who has benefited from therapy" to avoid seeking help for emotional distress.

Most of the wives in the study said that their husbands used some debunking theory to rationalize their refusal to see a therapist. They felt that the excuses were a cover-up for a deep-seated fear of therapy. Many husbands reacted as Arthur did when I suggested therapy earlier in the business crisis—by turning the tables and instructing their wives to go for therapy. "Nothing's wrong with me. You're the one who needs treatment." (Notice the projection.) When they finally dragged themselves to a therapist, they were already in the throes of the bonding crisis, heady with euphoria and poised for adultery, panic, and flight.

Adrienne Gioe, a therapist in Philadelphia specializing in couples work, believes that the pattern of husbands' walking out without making their intentions known in advance is the most prevalent scenario of divorce among higher-income families. Having supported many wives through the crisis, she is familiar with the conjunction of sudden abandonment and hard-boiled cruelty.

Gioe is encouraging about the prospects for preserving a marriage when a wife surmises that trouble is brewing—an affair or urge to leave—and is able to persuade her husband to attend therapy sessions. Resistant spouses often respond to an appeal to visit a therapist for the sake of the children.

To pave the way for acceptance, Gioe listens carefully to the reluctant husband at the opening meeting and makes sure that he is fortified by feeling that his point of view is being heard. Her methods reflect the influence of Ivan Boszormenyi-Nagy.

In Gioe's opinion, it is counterproductive for a dependent wife to become more subservient as her husband's demands escalate.

> The nicer the wife is, the more she conforms; the more she pleads, the more willing to do anything; the more angry the husband becomes and the more justified he feels in his course of action. The irony is that the wife becomes more valuable if she takes risks and establishes her independence. I've seen the same thing happen when the husband is the compliant partner.

Gioe notes that relationships become strained when one partner has a serious problem and the other backs away for fear that understanding carries an obligation to produce a remedy. Therapists can relieve this tension by helping couples discover that it is possible to acknowledge problems and not lose face or dissolve in panic over being unable to cure them. This "acknowledgment" can also deter rejection: So often the rejecter leaves to get away from the spouse who has become an unwelcome reminder of the problem that can't be solved.

When Arthur dismissed my concerns about him by suggesting that I see a therapist, I probably should have acted on his "advice." I could have said, "OK, I'll see a therapist but I won't talk only about myself. I will discuss my worry that you are overloaded with the burdens of the negotiations and not admitting how much of a toll it is taking on you." (At that time, I was so forgiving of his hostility and withdrawal that it wouldn't have occurred to me to mention that he was mistreating me.)

With my superficial knowledge of what to look for in a therapist, it would have been sheer accident if I had found someone like Betsy, trained to analyze unconscious defenses but open to helping couples and families. And even assuming I had stumbled upon a therapist with an authentically warm personality, a psychodynamic orientation, and great skills, it is legitimate to wonder whether anyone is capable of modifying the course of a relationship plagued by the delusions that go with bad-object rage. Having interviewed so many therapists, I think I can allay those doubts. But for the prognosis to improve, the wife-rejection syndrome will have to be spotlighted as a mental-health problem comparable to depression, alcoholism, or wife battering.

Not only did my husband indict and condemn our marriage before I knew we needed therapy, all six of the highly recommended psychoanalysts whom I visited after his announcement were of one opinion. They wanted me to accept treatment and flatly refused to conduct a session with both of us present, even though for at least a year after his departure, Arthur was willing to talk to me in the presence of a therapist. They insisted that it would be unethical to interfere with his personal therapist; I pleaded that it was unethical for his personal therapist not to be concerned about his family.

Finally, I turned to Dr. B, a psychiatrist recommended by a friend. He was not an analyst but a specialist in family and couples therapy and a professor of family psychiatry at a top-ranking medical school. Dr. B began our session by instructing Arthur to report all his grievances. It was in Dr. B's office that I first heard him sound so martyred, an exploited husband whose wife was always late for the movies and critical of his driving, and who "always got her way." Dr. B cut me off when I tried to interrupt to mention his tailgating or to ask how I could have dominated such an assertive, strong-minded husband.

This was my first glimpse of Arthur's agitation. I was alarmed at how distraught he became as the questioning proceeded. Just before Dr. B excused him, I thought he was going to break into tears.

Prior to that grilling by Dr. B, we had had a fairly pleasant dinner together during which Arthur seemed friendly and talkative. That was our last dinner. A week later, the man who sat across from me at lunch was grim and unyielding; he flinched when I touched him.

I went back to Dr. B to ask why he had spent the entire session goading Arthur to spill his grievances without once letting me speak. "I don't believe in wasting time. I was probing for signs of guilt. When I don't detect guilt, I conclude that therapy is useless because the marriage cannot be renegotiated." (It was many months later that Betsy supplied the salient information about guilt that was obviously unknown to Dr. B. From her I learned that a person consumed with narcissistic rage is outwardly impervious to guilt.)

Dr. B's blindness was compounded by his violation of what I learned later is a basic tenet of couples therapy. At the first session, the therapist should always try to elicit the couple's positive feelings for one another. "What was it about your husband or wife that first attracted you?"

After the debacle with Dr. B, a friend sent me to her psychoanalyst, a doctor with a significant reputation and no apparent hesitation about working with couples. Her assessment was that this was a "delicate case" for which she did not have time. She urged me to accept a referral to Mrs. S and to "put my trust in her."

Mrs. S was the psychoanalyst who proved to be a newcomer to bad-object rage. She opened most sessions by asking which of us wanted to speak first. Being the motivated spouse, I usually jumped in. Then Mrs. S would turn to Arthur and ask him to describe his reaction to my opening remarks. (How did you feel when your wife said she feels like a refugee?) It took me a while to realize that this was a formula guaranteed to put me on the defensive. He could convert whatever I said into an excuse for a gripe or for expressing disdain. I was a seated dart board.

Mrs. S defined her role as "listener." After two months, she made one useful observation: that Arthur seemed to have accumulated grievances without articulating them. For example, he had never told me that it infuriated him when I tapped other people's knowledge of topics on which he was well informed. He found it insulting that I would elicit opinions that might contradict him. I took this criticism as a facet of a latent competitiveness between us, and was frustrated that Mrs. S didn't encourage discussion.

Mrs. S did insist on my seeing her individually twice a week "because there's always a lot to talk about." That seemed expensive and unnecessary, but I felt pressured to cooperate.

It was a quirk of fate or memory that suddenly brought my friend Betsy back into focus. We had been out of touch for years, but I was reminded of her by a chance encounter with a woman from the same city in Texas who had been a childhood friend of hers. The reason I phoned instantly was that I knew that Betsy and her husband were deeply devoted to each other, having made career sacrifices to preserve their marriage. Perhaps she would not subscribe to the prevailing attitude that my marriage and our life were so disposable.

What proved more important than her personal commitment to love and marriage was her more modern approach to psychoanalytic therapy. She did not frown on helping couples and families or on being truthful with a patient.

By the time I poured out my story to Betsy, I was fairly well educated about the emotional consequences of low self-esteem. Ordinarily, I think she would have satisfied a patient's queries about wife rejection by comparing the husband's sudden aversion to an "allergy." Since she knew Arthur well enough to have judged him to be warm and appealing, she couldn't easily evade my questions about the refrigerated voice on the telephone. (It still hadn't occurred to me to describe him as angry.) Partly in astonishment, Betsy supplied the technical term: narcissistic rage.

Betsy wasn't anxious to provide any more information, but I was persistent, and fortunately for me, her professional code did not prohibit helping a friend.

It became increasingly clear that Mrs. S was content to listen indefinitely without exerting herself to make sense of what was transpiring between Arthur and me.

I pressed Betsy for more guidance. "What can I say to him?"

She advised me to quash any temptation to deliver interpretations or lay a guilt trip. "It will backfire if you make him feel guilty for abusing you," she counseled.

"If you say, 'You are punishing me,' he will feel attacked and will retaliate with countercharges. However, he may listen if you tell him how his behavior is making you *feel*: 'I feel as if I am being punished.' "

My growing impatience with Mrs. S's blank expression as she sat back listening to Arthur expanding on his false accusations and rewriting history to blame me for everything except his birthmarks prompted me to consider asking her to consult with Betsy, but I was afraid that, too, would backfire.

Finally, at one of our private sessions, during which Mrs. S was wrapped in a shawl and sniffling from a head cold, I took a deep breath and proposed that she discuss our case with the prominent psychoanalyst who had first recommended her to me.

Mrs. S grabbed for the box of tissues, clutched her nose, and shook her head. Her no was final.

With that impasse, I decided that I had no choice but to separate from Mrs. S. That wasn't easy. My doubts seemed to make her more attractive to Arthur, who probably relished the open invitation for target practice on me.

When I finally collected the courage to tell them both that I thought we should end the sessions since neither of us seemed to be benefiting, Mrs. S's response set me spinning. "After all, you did ask for couples therapy, not therapy for yourself." Arthur's rejoinder was even more startling. He reminded Mrs. S that on the phone she had asked him to attend a few sessions to help *me* get started with therapy. That's how I learned that Mrs. S had deceived both of us from the start.

My talks with Betsy encouraged my belief (or fantasy) that it wasn't too late for therapy to help, so I began casting around for a replacement for Mrs. S, preferably not Betsy since I couldn't gauge the effect of our prior friendship.

Having finally absorbed the harsh truth that Arthur was certifiably angry at me for reasons beyond his control and my comprehension, I decided to go headhunting for a therapist who excelled at helping people shed their anger. It seemed like an assignment for a voodoo healer. Was there a technique for getting the anger off me and putting it on something harmless, like a chicken? Maybe a hypnotist could help.

As usual, I was logical but misguided.

After some inquiry, I found a hypnotist who was also a psychoanalyst. He truly spooked me. My marital troubles made no impression at all; he wanted to treat *me* at the highest fee mentioned so far. If he had been selling memberships in a health club, I would surely have succumbed to the pressure and signed a contract. As it was, for fear of being entrapped on the telephone, I sent a letter to cancel the appointments he had entered in his date book.

There didn't seem to be any reliability about analysts so I proceeded to interview therapists who held Ph.D.s in clinical psychology, but were not necessarily trained in psychoanalysis. My search might have been more successful if I had made a different cut and sought only cooperative, psychodynamically oriented therapists without regard for whether they were full-fledged psychoanalysts.

My first visit was to a woman whose credentials were as a Family Therapist. She challenged my claim that my husband could have been such an exception to his dysfunctional family. It contradicted her premise that children always replicate the behavior of their original family. I tried to explain that Arthur aimed to excel where his parents had failed and gave the appearance of being a model father, husband, and community member until his emotional compactor overflowed.

Two psychologists who described themselves as couples therapists expounded similar points of view. They were convinced that anger begets anger. If my husband had stored anger, I must have contributed my share of provocation. One of them sounded only lukewarm when I inquired about his attitude toward marriage. "Well, *I'm* married," was all the testimonial he could summon.

Another psychologist, an exponent of "self psychology," did not oversell herself. She allowed that her expertise was really with individuals. Yet she was the one who was familiar with the "pop and dump" syndrome.

"Some men just explode and blame their wives for everything that ever happened to them from the day they were born." She couldn't explain this, but enough devastated wives had poured out their stories for her to predict that the accusations would get much worse. I found it ironic that she was more knowledgeable about the syndrome than the designated couples therapists.

Then a lunch with Arthur cut short the talent search. It left me so unhinged that I raced back to Betsy for refuge.

Prerejection, restaurants were associated in my mind with romantic evenings; a few stirred something akin to erotic feelings. Postrejection, all restaurants are a blur. I can't remember the names, let alone the food, of the restaurants where Arthur conducted our business. I can recall only the interior geography, the table coverings, and the direction I was facing as Arthur delivered his emotional karate chops. Also engraved in my memory is the choreography of his hands. When agitated, he would clench and unclench his fists in nervous succession; during one such meal his face twitched with anger, and his hands were out of sight under the table.

At this particular lunch, there was a robot sitting across from me, and he got right to the point. Since I had refused to sell our country house, he was now demanding exclusive possession. The eyes that had once danced with seduction were piercing and venomous. "You look as if you would prefer to see me dead." I hoped to be contradicted, but there was silence.

All of my foolish optimism vanished with the plate of untouched food that was whisked away by the waiter. I lost my nerve and composure and wept steadily for about a month. I woke up crying in the morning; tears blinded my eyes when I was driving. I couldn't eat and broke into sobs every time my mind played back the dialogue. My indispensable friend was out of town, and when I tried to tell other "friends" what had happened, they cut me off in midsentence.

My impulse was to flee. I hoped a friend, whom I cherished and whom I had supported through multiple crises, would invite me to visit for the weekend, but our phone call was over in five minutes, and that was my last voice contact with her. Reflecting on the way my friend had coped with illness, accident, and death, I realized that she rarely allowed her high spirits to sag. Tears were not in her repertoire.

The encounter with the robot, which took place about two months after I had suspended our conversations with Mrs. S, did not surprise Betsy.

"You don't understand," she admonished. "He must keep control. It probably infuriated him when you took the initiative and ended the sessions." When I had asked Betsy for advice on how best to break off with Mrs. S, she had demurred on the grounds that it would have been unethical to interfere with another therapist. (Silently, I wondered about the ethics of not alerting me to the hazards of my "taking control.")

I pleaded with Betsy to help me. "You're the only person who understands why Arthur is attacking me and who feels that I am owed some guidance and information." She volunteered to send me to a colleague, but I was emphatic about no more referrals. Fortunately, Betsy's professional code did not prohibit her from becoming our therapist.

One question that kept cropping up was the propriety of a therapist meeting with the two of us to talk about our relationship while Arthur was in individual treatment with Dr. X. The "ruling" was that it was OK for another therapist to see the two of us so long as Dr. X didn't object.

The truly potent question, however, was the one we all ignored. That was whether couples therapy could be productive while

Arthur was in individual treatment with a therapist who had no use for the family. I asked Betsy what approach she would use if she were treating someone in Arthur's state of mind. She said that she would work slowly and tactfully to gain the confidence of a patient with so much pent-up anger.

"It requires a lot of patience. The therapist can expect to be attacked and denigrated, although sometimes patients do the opposite: They show only their controlled false self. When I work with someone who is contemptuous of others but ingratiating toward me, I suspect that they are feigning cooperation and are really filled with toxins inside.

"Assuming that patients are motivated enough to stay in therapy, an alliance will eventually develop, and they will begin to project their anger onto the therapist." She grimaced at the thought, explaining that in the context of analysis, projections relating to the therapist are referred to as transference. "This can take a long time, but when they are able to experience repressed anger and to recover its source in childhood frustrations, they usually feel immense relief. It's pretty rough on the therapist when anger descends, but letting it out in the therapeutic relationship usually reduces the need to abuse others."

I was curious about how Betsy would handle a wife like me if a husband like Arthur had enlisted her help. "Would you hang up on your patient's wife the way Dr. X hangs up on me?"

"No, I would never do that. There is a problem, however, if your patient instructs you not to talk to his wife: You are honor bound to follow his wishes regarding confidentiality. Fortunately, no patient has ever refused me permission to speak to a spouse when I thought it was necessary.

"If I were treating somebody like Arthur, I would tell him that his wife had called, and ask consent to talk to her. We would discuss what I could say. I would urge him to agree to a joint meeting to talk things over. If he refused, I would press him to allow me to give her some guidance. I might say, 'Your wife seems very confused and upset. Don't you feel she is entitled to some help? Perhaps I could advise her to see a therapist to counsel her and your children.' "

"What would your attitude be toward working with the family?" I asked.

"Therapists disagree, but I prefer to work with the whole family in most situations, including this type of crisis. It's easier to monitor the projections and distortions. A patient can't manipulate and mislead the therapist if other members of the family are around to report the truth. Often a child will force the family to face their denial by revealing information the adults are withholding."

After that alarming lunch with the "robot," I really should have consulted a lawyer, but my actions were guided not by common sense or self-preservation but by an emotional imperative to expend every effort to reconstitute our marriage. (Many rejected wives have the choice between a therapist and lawyer made for them. If they are unlucky enough to live in a state that allows no-wait, no-fault divorces, their husbands may serve papers immediately. If they are unscrupulous, they can force their wives to file for divorce by the simple expedient of stopping support.)

I could not picture myself locked in legal combat with Arthur; moreover, I was terrified of being manipulated into being targeted as the person he needed to defeat to compensate for all the other defeats he had suffered during the business negotiations. Every fiber told me that the least Arthur owed me was respect for our past and honesty about his undoing of our marriage, a prerequisite that was about as realistic as expecting a cat to show respect for the sparrow before pouncing.

After much persuasion, Betsy agreed to serve as our mediator, if not as our therapist, and after modest persuasion, Arthur agreed to accept her services. I was braced for a second encounter with the robot and didn't realize until the "hour" was almost over and I steeled myself to look him in the eye that the murderous expression was gone. Betsy was performing a miracle: Arthur seemed almost cooperative when we left. I was amazed that Betsy was able to deliver on her theories. As far as I could tell, she had skillfully conveyed to Arthur a sense of being in control and thereby enhanced his comfort level. I tried to tell him that I felt like a parasite after that dreadful lunch, but he claimed not to understand what had upset me.

Betsy explained that sudden mood shifts are to be expected with this condition. It was her repeated references to "this" condition that prompted me to ask what "this" was. Does "this" behavior pattern have a name? Where can I read about "this"? When I pressed for answers, she insisted that she knew of no written information on "this" and couldn't even suggest a glossary term under which to look it up.

"You mean that therapists know that innocent spouses get clobbered like this and haven't even bothered to give it a name? No wonder there's no help available. No wonder everybody feels free to shun the victims."

Prodded by my insistence and her conscience, Betsy helped me devise the vocabulary to describe "this": wife rejection, bonding crisis, and Chernobyl effect. The language of "rejection" seemed appropriate because of the parallel to tissue rejection.

Betsy remained our therapist for about four months, until the customary August vacation, after which Arthur was no longer co-operating. He went on a trip with his girlfriend and started threatening to cut the amount of his monthly checks if I didn't go along with his demands to divide property.

As I have broadened my contacts and information on various approaches to therapy, I realize that I was exceptionally unlucky in my first encounters. It may be illusory to think that a knowledgeable, committed therapist would have made any difference, but it weighs heavily on my mind and heart that I never had the chance to find out.

Of course, therapy can be misused by spouses who have crossed the Rubicon of rejection. A husband sometimes enlists the services of a therapist to "take care" of his wife so he won't have to feel so guilty about dumping her. Sometimes a rejecting spouse will commandeer therapy sessions to mount an attack on the faithful spouse.

None of the writings on couples therapy I have reviewed have discussed helping a motivated spouse save the marriage *after* the other spouse has shut down (or cut off, as Murray Bowen refers to the equivalent of the Chernobyl effect). Reading between the lines, however, it's possible to predict that some of the approaches that are advocated would reduce the risk of a full-fledged crisis—

specifically those that help spouses open up about their neediness and examine their contributions to a projective identification.

Psychoanalyists, who have the most profound appreciation of what it feels like to be attacked as a bad object, have developed a reputation—not undeserved—for being casual toward marriages. Some analysts are indifferent, even hostile, to spouses; others, however, have expanded their horizons to working with couples and families.

The following is a sampling (obviously partial) of some of the theories of couples therapy that, judging from writings, interviews, conferences, and demonstrations, seem to recommend methods that would help a spouse reconstruct a battered self-image within the context of couples therapy, thus reducing the risk of resorting to wife rejection.

In identifying "narcissistic vulnerability" as the major cause of marital breakdown today, Marion Solomon has focused on the disturbance that seems to be at the root of wife rejection. Solomon, who teaches and practices "psychodynamic" couples therapy in Los Angeles, holds that couples should be approached as a separate specialty. Since the couple is really the patient, the methods derived from treating individuals or families are not necessarily applicable.

One of Solomon's goals is to help spouses discover "that a mate's [damaging] behavior and statements are [often] not meant as an attack but as a way of protecting against hurt."

Solomon notes that projections are always part of the presenting material and that projections can serve as trailblazers to guide the therapist to the specific fears and inadequacies the spouses are in the habit of evading by attributing them to the partner. "Handling projections requires going back and forth between partners, allowing anxious feelings to emerge without being pushed away or projected for as long as the partners can tolerate."

Murray Bowen has more to say about the operation of projective identification between spouses than most other theorists identified with the various schools of Family Therapy. (Although Bowen refers to "relationship fusion" and "emotional reactivity," these terms are close in concept to projective identification.)

The goal of the therapist is to help the client (whether an individual or a couple) achieve a successful balance between needing to be an individual and needing to be in a relationship.

In working with a couple, the therapist would try to help the husband and wife gain confidence in their ability to manage their own anxiety, and thereby lessen the need either to draw the mate into conflicts that arose in the family of origin or to insert a third party into a triangulation to take pressure off the pair.

If one spouse is reluctant to be in therapy, a Bowen-trained therapist would be willing to "coach" the more motivated spouse to work on differentiation of self in order to create a climate in which the partner would also learn to manage anxiety without projecting blame onto the relationship.

Tavistock in London, where the object relations school originated, has a long history of applying psychoanalytic insights to marital conflict. When the divorce rate climbed after World War II, Tavistock undertook to investigate the causes and to experiment with therapy for couples. A first and still highly valued book applying object relations insights to couples therapy, *Marital Tensions* by Henry Dicks, emerged from this project.

Back in 1967 Dicks was forthright in revealing what he knew about the pattern of one spouse relocating the despised part of himself in the partner and for that reason attacking the partner mercilessly. One of his innovations, still practiced today, is assigning two therapists to a couple so each spouse can identify with a positive parenting figure. (This can be expensive unless one therapist is a trainee.)

David and Jill Scharff, psychoanalysts who received training at Tavistock and work now in Washington, D.C., have written and lectured extensively on an approach to couples and family therapy that utilizes the insights of object relations.

Along with Solomon, the Scharffs borrow from Winnicott the concept of the therapist providing a "container" or stabilizing center to hold the conflict so it doesn't overwhelm the individuals. For them, a therapist who doesn't strive for insight is setting her or his sights too low. They recommend that therapists study the "counter-transference," or the emotions that the spouses evoke in the therapist, for clues to the content of the unconscious messages they are in the habit of sending each other.

Herbert Strean, a psychoanalyst in New York, has taken a deep interest in marital therapy. Among his numerous books is one devoted to marital therapy and another that elucidates patterns in extramarital affairs. He leaves no doubt in the reader's mind that to understand the truth of our relationships we must journey through the terrain of our individual and merged unconscious. As for adultery, it comes in many guises. Oftentimes, a spouse engages in an affair to take the pressure off the relationship by adding a third party. This need for triangulation can disappear in the course of working through personal discontents, insecurities, and demons in couples or individual therapy.

A writer on couples therapy who impresses as being theoretically and clinically attuned to preventing the conditions that lead to wife rejection is Daniel B. Wile of Oakland, California. He faults psychoanalytic therapy for the focus on diagnosing personality defects and criticizes behavioristic and systemic therapists for attempting to improve the way spouses treat each other without dealing with the feelings that cause them to be distancing or exploitive.

Wile cautions against confusing compatibility with intimacy. Whereas intimacy depends on being able to share thoughts and feelings, compatibility is more superficial, a sharing of interests only. The goal of therapy, according to Wile, should be to help a couple learn more about the feelings they suppress and the deprivations that lie dormant only to burst forth later as projected anger.

Margaret Golton, the therapist in University Heights, Ohio, who attributes rejection behavior to a takeover by the emotionally charged limbic system in the brain, has a unique approach to therapy with people who have a poorly defined sense of "self" and corresponding lapses in appreciating the separateness of "others." She forthrightly tells patients that their distress is caused by the lack of a "self" and that the deficiency can be remedied. She encourages them to perform tasks related to self-awareness and assessing strengths and weaknesses. These tasks are intended to reinforce and multiply connections with the brain that will strengthen the perception of one's own person and individuality.

Harville Hendrix, a psychotherapist in New York City, has written a guide for couples therapy titled *Getting the Love You Want*, in which he expresses optimism that marriages can be preserved with the help of therapy specifically geared to couples. His eclectic approach incorporates spiritual values and insights from all branches of psychoanalytic thinking. The threshold step is facilitating an acceptance by each spouse of his or her own wounded child and of the wounded child suffering inside the mate. Then the therapist tries to help the couple heal their childhood wounds and identify and resolve their "complementary defenses."

Jurg Willi is a Swiss psychoanalyst whose writings on couples therapy reflect an awareness of the complexity of the unconscious interplay between spouses and a perspective on therapy that includes respect and help for the couple as individuals and as a unit.

At the same time that I hold out hope that this information will help others, I must confess that it is of no use to me now. My husband has found ways to punish that ensure that I will initiate communication only out of dire necessity. Active listening helps me to state that necessity in the least accusatory fashion—"Did you forget to send the check?"—or crystallize the intent of his behavior—"I'm wondering why you feel it's all right to drain my savings to pay for a divorce I don't want." (That was my last conversation on the phone and it was six months ago.)

You can't follow the rule to avoid making someone feel guilty when every word and action seems custom-calculated to hurt and deprive you. Even worse, there's a feedback loop. Since your very existence is a reminder of the guilt, they punish you for being the ghost who reminds them of their unconscionable behavior. Thus a blackout is the only way to protect yourself from the emotional attacks, and that's only possible if you have no children living at home. I have no idea how I would survive emotionally if I had to withstand the humiliation for the sake of dependent children.

Only a lawyer could help me negotiate the next stage. I had no choice but to join the company of women who have had to battle their husbands over money, property, and custody, a marital outcome I never could have foreseen because *my* husband was such "a nice guy."

Thus began my exposure to a comparatively new form of institutionalized exploitation of rejected wives, the no-fault divorce, borrowed from the rules promulgated for automobile accidents. It's bad enough when therapists turn their backs on rejected wives, but neutrality on the part of the legal system deprives rejected wives of the only meaningful form of compensation for their losses—enough money to maintain their standard of living.

9

"There Is No Penalty to Me for Leaving You This Way."

▼

If the reformers who drafted the liberalized divorce laws had set out to design rules to vanquish abandoned spouses, they could not have improved on the Uniform Matrimonial Code that was adopted in 1974 as a model for state matrimonial laws.

The authority to regulate marriage and divorce is constitutionally reserved for the state legislatures. Not too long ago, many states had highly restrictive divorce laws that required proof of wrong-doing such as adultery or physical or mental abuse on the part of one of the spouses. Barriers to divorce began to fall in the sixties along with the other restrictions on individual freedom. Popular opinion favored freer divorce laws so couples would no longer be forced to remain technically married when they were physically and emotionally separated.

To review trends and guide the changes in matrimonial law, a commission comprised of prestigious scholars and practitioners was formed and assigned the task of drafting a new uniform code, a model law that could be recommended to the states and serve as an incentive for the states to harmonize their divorce laws. (Such commissions are formed from time to time when the legal community agrees on the need for modernization of a major body of law.) Led by California, which adopted a matrimonial law based on no-fault premises even earlier, in 1969, most states have incorporated some or all of the provision of the 1974 Uniform Matrimonial Code.

The Code does away with obstacles to divorce. It reads:

The court shall enter a decree of divorce if the court finds that the marriage is irretrievably broken, if the finding is supported by evidence that

(i) the parties have lived separate and apart for a period of more than 180 days next preceding the commencement of the action, or

(ii) there is serious mental discord adversely affecting the attitude of one or both of the parties toward the marriage.

This means that in states that have adopted the equivalent of this provision of the Code, a husband or wife can walk out and six months later file for divorce, contending that the marriage he or she broke up has broken down. Evidence of separation is not even necessary; one spouse can simply claim marital discord as justification for his or her demand for a no-questions-asked divorce.

The only test the Code would apply is whether the marriage is irretrievably broken: "A finding of irretrievable breakdown is a determination that there is no reasonable prospect of reconciliation," which, of course, is based on one spouse's claim, regardless of whether that spouse is the one who has abruptly or systematically sabotaged the marriage.

To implement the concept of "no fault," the states have adopted a ground for divorce that is variously termed "irretrievable or irremediable breakdown," "irreconcilable differences," or "incompatibility." The exact same standard is applied whether the couple has been married for two months or forty-two years and whether they are childless or the parents of enough children to fill a station wagon.

This is a typical example of the pendulum swinging. Restrictive divorce laws were universally condemned for denying individuals the right to end a truly unhappy or crippling marriage. Instead of a moderate liberalization to allow for orderly dissolution of incompatible marriages, the "reforms" have removed all barriers to divorce as if social value were no longer vested in preserving marriages. In the no-fault era, marriage is treated as a business partnership, to be broken by either party as speedily as one spouse can coerce the other into a financial settlement.

Lawyers and judges felt that disputes over fault contributed to the vitriolic trading, inflation, and inventing of charges that accompanied divorces in which "fault" weighed in the outcome of the proceedings. They reasoned that divorces could be more amicable if the proceedings were made less adversarial by blocking out all questions pertaining to which party was at fault in the breakdown of the marriage.

Instead of moving to an intermediate position of encouraging mutual divorce when spouses are in agreement, no fault traded one radical position for another: It granted immunity for being injurious to your spouse and nothing for being loyal, supportive, and altruistic. No-fault seems to be saying that human nature is so low that no husband or wife can be judged to have behaved with honor and caring in their marriage.

Marion Solomon, who practices couples therapy in Los Angeles, criticizes the permissiveness of no-fault in allowing one party to request dissolution of the marriage. "The current divorce laws reflect cultural values. Personal happiness takes precedence over commitment to another."

One serious shortcoming of no-fault procedures is that innocent spouses are denied a hearing and compensation for wrongdoing. Even documented physical abuse is whitewashed.

Another shortcoming of the no-fault concept is that it dispenses with any obligation on the part of the dissatisfied spouse to attempt to fix the marriage before scuttling it.

The injustice that most rankles the victims of wife rejection is the ease with which their husbands were able to manipulate no-fault laws to gain the offensive and call the plays.

The practicing lawyers among the framers of the uniform law must have represented clients who told of sudden abandonment and sudden rage, but they probably dismissed these allegations as hysterical or exaggerated. Who can blame lawyers for not wanting to know that a decent, upstanding citizen—a nice guy whom everybody likes—might resolve his emotional crisis by tackling his wife to the ground as if she were the quarterback on the opposing team?

The facts of wife rejection—that some marriages break down inside one partner's head—contradict the convenient fiction of no-fault: that both parties are mutually responsible for the breakdown of a marriage.

So habituated are judges and matrimonial lawyers to angry clients that they are likely to turn a deaf ear to the fine distinction between an angry attacking spouse and an angry defending spouse and a blind eye to the frequency with which the attacking spouse is also the family treasurer. No-fault not only fails to discipline the aggressor, it gifts him or her with the whole courthouse.

This pattern of overprotecting attacking husbands and underprotecting defending wives seems ingrained in the legal system. To change attitudes toward disadvantaged spouses requires recognition of just how one-sided marital breakup can be.

Since lawmakers are not sensitive enough to one-sided abuse to declare even major offenses like physical battering off limits to no-fault, how could they be expected to recognize the fault in sudden abandonment? Well, a first step would be to give sudden, malicious abandonment a label such as *aggressive abandonment* so it will be grouped with other forms of marital misconduct.

Aggressive abandonment—leaving without warning, provocation, or effort to conciliate and without making appropriate financial and social provisions for the abandoned spouse and children— could be classified as wrongdoing that disqualifies the abandoner from initiating a one-party divorce and that will draw penalties in the financial settlement. The reason such a minimum standard of conduct would be worth the price of the legal arguments involved in enforcing it is that it addresses the specific injuries that abandoners and abusers routinely inflict on their spouses.

In a book entitled *Days Like This*, a rejected wife, a resident of Connecticut who calls herself Phyllis Gillis, reports in detail the hardships that befell her from the moment her husband renounced their eleven-year marriage until the divorce decree was signed two years later.

Phyllis Gillis represents a more broadly defined group of rejected wives who are surely more numerous than the group I studied. If asked to describe their husbands before the sudden departures, these women would not have highlighted their ethics or humanity. Gillis knew her husband to be a tough and perhaps crafty negotiator, someone you would prefer not to tangle with. A person in the habit of driving hard bargains in his business is liable to treat his wife the same way if she falls outside his charmed circle.

Over an intimate dinner to celebrate her birthday, Phyllis's husband delivered a strange accusation: that *she* was suicidal. A few days later he took out an insurance policy on her life. Why would a husband declare his wife suicidal when she had never given any indication of such despair? And why take out insurance when suicide is never covered?

The mystery can be unraveled only if you know something about the code of projection. When unacceptable thoughts are spilling over during an attack of rage and guilt, one way to get rid of them is to attribute them to a surrogate, someone who is very close, such as a spouse. The person who was feeling suicidal might well have been the husband. The accuser might be describing himself. A clue would be the attitude of the accuser. If a husband were really concerned that his wife was suicidal, wouldn't he be worried and sympathetic rather than caustic and castigating?

(During one of those terrifying luncheons, Arthur upbraided me for "being scared out of your wits during the business crisis." He was right that I was quaking some of the time, and to the extent that he could read my fears, I'm sure I added to his tension. But why was my weakness something to be scorned? Probably because he was so disapproving of his own fright.)

The specific conflict that sparked rejection by Phyllis's husband seemed to be his opposition to her ambition for an independent livelihood. This would hardly rank as a major trauma—unless the husband was someone whose stability depended on being dominant and keeping his wife under his thumb.

After many false starts, Phyllis devised a plan for starting a small business that seemed to overcome her husband's objections. However, even the extreme maneuver of forcing her to incorporate her business as a subsidiary of his did not seem to satisfy his need to maintain control.

Returning home late from a "business meeting" one night, he announced that he would be moving—the next day—into an apartment he had taken with a neighbor, who at that very moment was delivering a parallel message to her husband.

Phyllis depicted her husband as totally in command as he laid out his plans to trade her in for an improved model, a woman who was a full-time homemaker. If his words had not been so bruising, Phyllis might have noticed signs of concealed panic. A posture of being tough and in charge can be deceptive; sometimes, as we have noted, it serves as a cover-up to mask anxiety.

When her husband returned a few days later to pick up his belongings, Phyllis observed that "he seemed to want to get away from me as quickly as possible, as though I had some contagious disease." This aversion to her physical presence has the earmarks of the Chernobyl effect—fleeing from his wife because she is contaminated with memories or feelings he wished to blot out—but like other rejected wives, Phyllis could not recognize symptoms of a syndrome that was unknown to her.

That no-fault procedures are monumentally unfair to abandoned wives was tacitly acknowledged by her husband. As he barked out his decisions the night of his announcement, he added, "I am leaving you this way because the law says I can. . . . A no-fault divorce means no one is at fault. There is no penalty to me for leaving you in this way."

Another quote from Phyllis's husband captures the self-justifying projection that seems to be the universal excuse of the rejecting husbands for continuing to persecute their deposed wives: "You are angry that I am happy and you will try and take your anger out on me by getting even."

This prophecy seems to operate like a persecutory delusion. From all accounts, there was no basis for predicting vindictiveness or obstruction on Phyllis's part, since she was not opposing the divorce. It appears to be an outright transfer of guilty and vengeful feelings to his wife. Once her husband convinced himself that his wife was the one harboring feelings of guilt and desire for revenge, it would follow that she *deserved* the social and financial punishment he was inflicting on her. Whatever she did to defend herself (or whatever her lawyer did on her behalf) would be interpreted as "getting even"—retaliation instead of self-defense.

On one occasion her husband told her that he would have left her even if he had not found a new mate. Such urgency is consistent, of course, with a bonding crisis. If the pain is severe enough, the rejecting husband *may* leave in haste even before finding a new attachment.

This wholesale rejection delivers not one but three knockout blows: first, the abandonment; second, the insult of being replaced by a new and supposedly more desirable mate; and third, the brutal message that you count for nothing in the eyes of your former spouse. Not only have you lost your attractiveness as a "good object," you are being extruded as a "bad object," as posing a threat of danger and disorder and deserving of contempt and banishment.

On another occasion Phyllis's husband told her that he hadn't been able to communicate with her because she thought only of her own needs.

That statement riveted me to the page. That had been *my* husband's complaint at the end of a telephone conversation the day before! As always, my first reaction was to reflect on his criticism, in this case, *my* selfishness, and as an afterthought to check his accusation against our history. I remembered which one of us had stopped communicating, and which one of us had been ignoring the other's needs. It was only after I hung up that I was able to decode the projections and then only because I now store a template for projection up front in my brain.

Understanding the content of an accusation to be a projection is no help in answering it. It is impossible to disprove these distortions, which are repeated over and over after wife rejection and which coalesce in feelings of self-pity and victimization and are used to justify retaliation in the form of stripping the rejected spouse, emotionally and financially.

Like other rejected wives, Phyllis discovered that no penalty would be levied against her husband for stopping his voluntary checks and cutting off her utilities at the same time he was expending lavish sums on furnishings, vacations, and gifts for his "wife-elect."

On the day of an ice storm, there were successive calls from the oil company, the electric company, and the insurer of her automobile, with the identical message. They had received letters from her husband stating that he would no longer be responsible for the bills and instructing them to return his deposits.

According to the representative of the oil company, the utilities have no choice but to comply even though they are aware of the pattern of husbands enlisting the utilities as accomplices in pressuring their wives into a disadvantageous divorce settlement.

There is a legal remedy for a wife whose husband stops support or cuts off basic services when a divorce action is pending. If she can still afford lawyer's fees, she can request a court hearing for the purpose of ordering him to pay interim support and maintenance while the financial settlement is being negotiated.

This procedure of asking for temporary relief while a motion is pending poses many hardships for an abandoned wife. In too many courts, the sudden cutoff of income is not treated as a true emergency. It can take weeks, even months, to calendar a hearing, and postponements are routinely granted at the request of the husband's lawyer. Furthermore, the temporary amount awarded by the court—invariably at the low end of the scale—is taxable and may convert to the permanent figures for support and maintenance in the final settlement. Another hardship is that these motions require rapid response and substantial paperwork. The insolvent wife will be billed for every minute her lawyer spends interviewing her, investigating the finances, preparing the papers, arguing the case, even standing around the courthouse waiting for the case to be called.

Since no penalty attaches to stopping support, these sudden cutoffs are the weapon of choice of an unscrupulous husband. The court seems to be issuing husbands an open invitation to use its facilities to postpone paying obligations to their families and to lower wives' expectations and prospects for a fair settlement.

Unless the husband is superrich, the courts do not credit the wife and the children with equal entitlement to a comparable life-style. Arrears are customarily wiped out, and there is no consideration of the wife's right to collect interest on the involuntary loan extended to the husband during the period he withheld support.

The only enforceable limits on how much pressure an unscrupulous husband is permitted to apply are set by the law. If heavy penalties were imposed for harassment, there is a good chance that the majority of rejecting husbands/fathers would desist, their compulsion to hurt their wives stopping just short of being in contempt of court—an offense that can send the accused to jail.

There is a penalty that legislators adopt when they want to discourage violations that society takes seriously: They insert provisions calling for treble damages. Economic blackmail might not look so inviting to a rejecting husband if he ran the risk of having to pay his wife (and children) three times the amount withheld.

Expectations that a wife can bounce back—like one of those push-over bounce-back toys—after rejection and find a terrific job and a new set of friends are blind to the reality of how emotionally and intellectually disabling it is to lose your husband as a friend and acquire him as an enemy. Even women with lower expectations of their husbands and greater drive for autonomy than the wives I interviewed have found it a paralyzing experience.

A rejected wife could easily spend a year or two in a semicomatose depression. It hurts so much. However, there is no respite to assuage her grief if she is unlucky enough to live in a no-wait, no-fault state. She may have to mount a defense to her husband's petition for divorce while still in a condition of shock. Regardless of where she lives, she will be thrust into the role of protector and therapist for some very heartsick children. She will also be hounded to get a job by the same husband who forbade her to work while he was dominating the household.

The Gillis book provides invaluable documentation of just how damaging a previously devoted parent can be to his or her child after a bonding crisis. Phyllis portrays her husband as a good father who could have been expected to maintain a warm relationship with their six-year-old son even after setting up housekeeping with a wife-elect.

It didn't work out that way, and I doubt that it ever would. It seems doubtful that a person inflamed to the point of waging war against his wife could have the empathy to nurture his child.

By the same token that no-fault advises the courts to be impervious to spousal abuse and cruelty, it supports judges in disregarding abuse and cruelty in custody decisions. Since judges have been known to award custody to fathers who have been convicted of violence against their wives, it is not surprising that judges fail to question the prognosis for loyalty to children of fathers who abandon their wives and proceed to sue for custody.

Like the other husbands whose rejecting behavior ended in divorce, Phyllis's husband never negotiated from the stance of a person wishing to end his marriage with a degree of justice and mutual respect, but from that of an unscrupulous opponent who arrogantly defies rules of law and decency.

Most of the criticism of no-fault has centered on whether the division of property and assets is fair to the partner who worked for lower or no wages. There has been little challenge to the philosophy of neutrality. Did the lawmakers and policymakers intend to be neutral between breaking up and preserving marriages? Did they intend to empower the unfaithful partner?

If we still value marriage and responsible parenting, then the casual endorsement of divorce that goes by the name of no-fault deserves rethinking. Some kind of standard should emerge obliging partners in a long marriage to make a conscientious effort at repair, preferably with the help of a third party—a clergyman, a doctor, a therapist—before breaking away unilaterally. (In other words, if you feel yourself turning angry and rejecting toward your spouse, you should bring your anxiety to a mediating professional before filing for a divorce.)

This is not the kind of requirement that can be written into law and enforced. Compliance is too easily faked. However, it mocks justice to allow a spouse who has not observed these elementary responsibilities to initiate a divorce and label it no-fault.

At the most, this cooling-off period would save some marriages called off in haste or ecstasy, since we know that some of the husbands wake up from their anger as if from amnesia, anxious to restore their marriage and family life. At the least, it would reserve some options and leverage for the abandoned spouse.

An agreement for a mutual divorce would be preferable for ending brief marriages without children or marriages in which both spouses agree on the incompatibility, even marriages in which the separating spouse is responsible and respectful—but no-fault should be spelled "no accountability" when it is applied to relationships characterized by physical abuse, substance abuse, nonsupport, adultery, and aggressive abandonment—behavior that is too damaging or malicious to dissolve into the no-fault language of "irreconcilable differences," "irretrievable breakdown," or "incompatability."

Aggressive abandonment spotlights a category of spousal abuse that materializes late in a marriage—beginning just before and persisting long after abandonment. To repeat what has been said before but what is always difficult to absorb: A husband who abandons his wife to escape an internal bonding crisis often develops an exorbitant urge to hurt and blame her. Because everyone expects divorcing spouses to treat each other badly, this lapse into *one-sided* cruelty has been lost among the multitude of vindictive tactics that show up in a contested divorce.

While laws cannot stop a husband from *feeling* entitled to "get even" with his wife for imagined wrongs, they can discourage him from *acting* on those feelings of persecution.

Laws, for example, can say that a spouse who abandons without warning or provocation has to wait a long time before he or she can sue for divorce without gaining consent of the spouse. They can rule out joint custody for a spouse who abandons and harasses and can mandate extra protection for spouses and children who are abandoned and harassed. They can enforce the parent's obligation to provide financially for his family by imposing stiff penalties for withholding support or canceling basic services and insurance. More muscular laws would make it clear that a change of address does not cancel responsibilities to the family left behind.

If matrimonial laws were amended in this fashion, a husband on the brink of rejection would no longer get the green light from his lawyer. The attorney would have to advise him that if his conduct can be construed as aggressive abandonment, he will not be permitted to file for divorce or to seek joint custody without his wife's consent. A conscientious lawyer would also have to warn a prospective client that he or she could face fines for withholding support or rearranging assets in anticipation of divorce.

In the course of advocating for reform in the divorce laws, Max

Rheinish, a lawyer and sociologist in Chicago, traced the attitudes and codes for dissolving marriages from ancient times to the present. He rightly noted that lenient divorce laws are not the cause of marital breakdown. What he missed is the extent to which the rules of divorce set the parameters for how much injury the divorcing spouse is permitted to inflict on the repudiated spouse and family.

What the "reformers" did not predict was that no-fault would foster expensive, spurious challenges to custody and would deprive abused and abandoned wives and children of the half-a-leg they had to stand on when fault counted.

10

No-Fault Impartiality: A Battered Wife and Her Custody Battle

▼

I have just returned from a custody hearing: a routine contest of wits if you are a lawyer, a momentous contest to decide your child's future if you are the parent. Watching a physically assaultive husband take advantage of no-fault to bid unashamedly for custody of their three-year-old toddler was like watching a demonstration of ultimate audacity.

I attended the hearing to give moral support to Nina, a young woman whose marriage disintegrated in the split second her husband changed from admiring to accusatory to violent. The transformation from approval to denigration was as swift as it was lasting, without the interim periods of "honeymoon" between bouts of abuse that are commonly reported by victims of battering. Over a two-year period, Nina's husband struck her eight times: half of those times she was thrown to the ground, and, consistent with rejection, he never apologized, never admitted that he had done anything wrong.

Although Nina did not fit the criteria for inclusion in my study of sudden endings to long marriages, having been married for seven instead of the minimum of ten years and having already acquired some doubts about her husband's character, she had suffered the injury of aggressive abandonment and was about to be tested as a witness in a proceeding that did not honor her credentials as a loving mother, brilliant scholar, and all-round gentle woman.

Without question, Nina had blinded herself to some troubling incongruities in her husband's personality, particularly in the way he related to dependency. Three years earlier, when their daughter, Gail, was born, Howard had seemed so full of joy that she felt justified in overlooking a few blind spots that didn't mesh with being a devoted or sensitive parent.

One of Howard's blind spots was a postpartum tendency to get very angry with Nina when he couldn't control her; another was to push the limits of safety with Gail. According to Nina, his mask of calm reasonableness dropped off so suddenly that she reacted by pretending that it hadn't happened. Preparatory to her weekly expedition to the supermarket, Nina was strapping Gail into her infant seat when Howard rushed over and for no apparent reason ordered her to switch cars from the one she usually drove to his, which was not equipped with an infant seat.

Nina protested that it was illegal to drive with a baby not fastened into a proper infant seat, but Howard wouldn't listen and became enraged as she got ready to leave. "He yanked me away from the car, knocked me down on the driveway, and pinned me there for what seemed like several minutes."

My mind balked at picturing the scene: this tall, handsome, supremely confident man with the build of a fullback overpowering his petite wife who can't weigh more than a hundred pounds after a big meal.

This was the debut of a new and terrifying Howard who never said he was sorry and who converted their marriage into a "battlefield where he had to prove that he was always right and I was always wrong. Soon thereafter, he moved out of our bedroom into the spare room, put a bolt on the door and started practicing yoga and meditation."

Nina endured continuous verbal deprecation and seven more episodes of physical violence for the sake of a futile effort to reawaken Howard's respect and affection. Over Howard's objections, she visited several therapists and joined a battered-women's group. She took their advice and phoned the police so there would be a record of reporting his assaults. After two years of physical and emotional abuse, peaked by another attack in front of Gail, Nina moved out. "I was less concerned for myself than for Gail. I couldn't allow her to witness another assault.

On the surface Howard was a fit parent, but several incidents caused Nina to question his trustworthiness. There were moments when he showed a comparable need to impose his will on Gail, such as the time he held her down screaming in order to wash lipstick marks off her face.

There was also an emerging pattern of being careless about safety, as if he wanted to prove that a small child could take care of herself. He was sitting on the shore of a lake fully clothed, about one hundred feet away from Gail, when she wandered into water over her head; he wouldn't strap her into the stroller when she was so small that there was danger she would bounce out; he let her toddle around the supermarket when it was unsafe for her to be anywhere but in the cart; and once he let her wander on her own and get lost at the zoo.

Nina was alarmed by each of these lapses but took them to be exceptions until the evidence accumulated of a behavior pattern that seemed to be characterized by a compulsion to be careless. In this respect, his treatment of their baby was not too different from his handling of their dogs.

"Once Howard got annoyed at one of our dogs for barking and grabbed him up by the scruff of the neck and bounced him on the floor. Another puppy was killed by a car after I had pleaded with Howard not to let her outside alone because she was too young to know the lawn from the street. He blamed the dog for not being smart enough to stay out of the road."

The way Howard acted after that first assault was consistent with the wife-rejection sequence minus a departure. There was a sudden, angry (not elated) rejection followed by a sustained offensive against the wife, substitution of a new bond (to Eastern mysticism, not a lover), and separation (extra business trips, long time-outs for religious rituals, his own bedroom). This was aggressive abandonment while remaining technically in the marital abode.

Nina's departure, by contrast, had nothing in common with aggressive abandonment, since she had given plenty of notice, had extended herself to repair the relationship, and had gotten nothing but provocation in return.

She was actually hoping that separation would elicit a peacemaking gesture, but Howard was spoiling for war. He chose his weapons well: a zero balance in their joint checking account and a petition for a no-fault divorce incorporating a demand for immediate custody of Gail. Nina was abandoned to support herself and their daughter on her $19,000 teaching fellowship while Howard recruited top legal talent, a perk that comes with a substantial six-figure income. His warning to Nina that she would need pockets as deep as Rockefeller's to fight him seemed like an extra dose of sadism.

While many lawsuits originate with a vendetta, it's hard to imagine one with less merit than this crude attempt to challenge custody.

The hearing dragged on for five days, spread over a period of several months, even though it was established on the opening day that Nina had been the principal caregiver from the moment Gail was born; that Howard was no longer supporting the child whose custody he sought; and that his long hours and frequent business trips would subject Gail to unconscionable amounts of time with sitters or day care if he were to gain custody.

Highlights of the testimony included Howard denying his assaults on Nina—it was only a shove and a grab, not a punch and a hammerlock; a nursery-school director depicting Nina as an exemplary parent; a sitter revealing that Gail had told her that her Daddy had hit her Mommy: and a child psychiatrist (expert witness) reporting his assessment that Nina was an exceptionally good mother and Gail an exceptionally thriving child. (Howard refused to be evaluated.) That seemed like enough evidence for the judge to halt the proceedings and settle the custody issue, but no, he wanted to give both sides a full hearing.

I observed the judge listening intently when Howard introduced evidence of "negligence" on Nina's part: He told of coming home from a business trip and finding the baby with a diaper rash. In one breath Howard scolded Nina for not giving enough dinner parties and not spending enough time cleaning the house; in the next, he ridiculed her for taking too long to obtain her Ph.D. (How many candlelight meals did he expect his battered wife to prepare, and how was she supposed to concentrate on her research with her husband on such a rampage?)

Nina's lawyer reminded the judge that false charges are hard to disprove. I was repelled by the mocking contempt in Howard's voice, particularly as he described racing to pick up Gail at nursery school a month before—after the custody petition had been filed—because she had developed a fever and the teachers couldn't locate Nina, who was undergoing medical tests.

Nina had told me earlier about his abdication when Gail fell ill at the age of seven weeks. Fearing a life-threatening disease, the doctors determined that they would have to perform some delicate diagnostic procedures and wanted Nina to summon her husband—even dialed the number and handed her the phone—because they felt both parents were needed. Howard said, "Oh, *you* can take care of that, Nina," and left her to manage their baby, her fright, and the hospitalization all by herself.

Nina asked her lawyer, who seemed skillful and effective at some moments and somewhat inept at others, how he thought the judge was leaning. He declined to predict the outcome and warned of a tendency to mistakenly interpret proceedings in your favor. That sent a stab of fear to my innards, which I didn't mention to Nina.

During the lulls I was preoccupied with calculating the cost to Nina of this vindictive suit. Assuming the obvious, that Howard was going to stay on the offensive, there would be another series of hearings to set temporary support and then protracted negotiations to reach a financial settlement.

Nina said that she hated accepting money from her father, whose pockets were the size of a high-school principal's, but really had no choice. "I could lose Gail."

The psychiatrist who had evaluated her parenting came over at the end of long grilling by Howard's attorney with a compassionate apology: "I'm sorry, Nina, but I'm afraid I can't help you contain the costs: Your husband's lawyer is going to nitpick at my report."

While Nina entertained some hope of recovering the legal fees in the settlement, there were no guarantees.

Arriving for what was scheduled to be the last hearing, I scanned the room for Nina. When I finally caught sight of her, I realized why my first sweep had missed her: She looked so shrunken from her usual poised self. It was more than the dark circles under her eyes. As I put my arms around her to give her a hug, I realized that she was shaking uncontrollably.

There was barely enough time for a whispered conversation in the corridor outside. Nina couldn't hold back the tears as she allowed that she had been keeping her composure by never admitting to herself that Howard could win custody. Now she was confronted with the incredible fact that "Howard is getting such a full hearing on his false charges that the judge could be considering the inconceivable: taking a daughter from her mother who has been the primary caregiver every day of her life and giving her to a father who is careless about safety and incapable of empathizing with a child. You know that if Howard ever got custody, he would use it to clamp control on me forever."

Throughout the hearing I felt a level of combustible tension that reminded me of waiting at a hospital for news of the outcome of a loved one's surgery.

It was a cliffhanger, but in the end the judge awarded custody to Nina with generous visitations for Howard. Her lawyer did not want to raise Howard's breaches of elementary safety as a reason for limiting visitation for fear of damaging Nina's standing with the judge. This was the kind of "victory" that brought relief but no triumph. It felt more like an accident averted by such strokes of good luck as a generous father, a decent judge, and a competent lawyer.

To me, this hearing demonstrated the ascendancy of the parent with the deep pockets and the well-oiled internal keep-away catapult, the defense of repulsing all criticism by issuing a steady barrage of accusations. Always on the attack, Howard never had to defend his actions. With his repetitions of trivial complaints and guilt-free denial of his wife's testimony regarding physical assaults and compromises with safety, he compelled the court to take him seriously as a candidate for custody and, in so doing, depleted Nina's emotional and financial reserves for the forthcoming battles over money.

Commenting on the terror of being a mother defending against a father's spiteful, compulsive battle for custody, Phyllis Chesler, who documented widespread abuse of custody suits in *Mothers on Trial*, notes that it is "more psychologically devastating to be tormented or betrayed by an intimate than a stranger. Many mothers were paralyzed by ex-husbands who continually threatened to destroy or 'murder' them psychologically. They couldn't believe that husbands could treat them as 'strangers' or 'enemies,' and not as the mothers of their children."

How would restrictions on unilateral divorce and penalties for aggressive abandonment have helped Nina?

Nina was certainly trapped by the worst aspects of no-fault. Leaving home to escape physical and mental abuse proved self-defeating. Her husband grabbed the no-fault option as an opportunity to change the venue for his assaults from the living room to the courtroom. The no-fault petition had the effect of giving her husband a license to terrorize her for close to six months with the fear that he might succeed in legally kidnapping Gail.

Nina's self-protective departure, which was intended as pressure on her husband to mend his ways, could have been distorted by her husband into grounds for charging abandonment. Even though she fled for safety, he could have claimed abandonment and exploited this opening with the same tenacity he applied to custody. However, he might not have been so ready to harass her with a custody suit if he knew that the court would be influenced by the cumulative evidence that pointed to him as the violator of the marriage.

Custody is generally adjudicated separately to avoid contamination by the financial issues in the divorce. It seems appropriate to separate custody from finances, but not from fault. A father who has been charged with physical assaults, aggressive abandonment, and emotional cruelty in the petition for divorce might lack the credibility to swagger into court to demand custody.

Giving aggressive abandonment—leaving suddenly and showing callous disregard for the abandoned spouse—the bad name it deserves might stimulate a review of the standards for awarding custody and alimony. The rules governing custody seem blind to the commonsense linkage between mistreating a spouse and mistreating children.

The no-fault pivot toward impartiality more or less negated the reforms in custody that were in the offing in 1973 when an influential book entitled *Beyond the Best Interests of the Child* was published. Advocating an overhaul in our attitudes toward custody, the three authors—Joseph Goldstein, Anna Freud (daughter of Sigmund Freud), and Albert Solnit, a professor of law, a psychoanalyst, and a child psychiatrist-psychoanalyst, respectively—argued that decisions on custody should be guided by concern for the welfare of the child, not the rights of the parents, and advocated that custody be awarded more or less automatically to the"psychological parent," the parent to whom the child is most closely bonded.

Unfortunately, the authors went further and recommended that the custodial parent control visitation, advice that flies in the face of the universal preference for both parents remaining involved with the children and the general consensus that it is virtually impossible to enforce support from the noncustodial parent without granting visitation.

The value of introducing the concept of aggressive abandonment would be in setting a standard for reasonable conduct during separation and divorce and serving notice on spouses who are bent on dumping and running that they will be judged by their behavior toward the spouse they want to divorce.

Abandonment by the breadwinner really should be treated as a family emergency necessitating intervention by the court, the only authority over a husband who suddenly repudiates his responsibilities to his family. Victims ought to be able to go to court on their own, without hiring a lawyer, to obtain an order compelling the breadwinner to meet his customary financial obligations to the family.

Some voices have been raised in criticism of the uneven contests and the unfair financial outcomes that emerge from divorces litigated without regard for either party's innocence or malevolence.

After comparing matrimonial laws in the United States and various countries of Northern Europe, Mary Ann Glendon, professor at Harvard Law School, found American law wanting in protection for families. According to Glendon, our governmental programs provide fewer as-of-right services for children, and our divorce laws demand less of parents when a marriage breaks up. Glendon wonders how the term no-fault can be applied to a divorce granted at the request of one spouse, and she perceives an anti-family bias: No-fault makes it unsafe for a parent to stay home to raise the children.

The message of no-fault is that a husband can tear up a marital contract with a "clause" calling for a division of labor between the spouses—husband as wage earner, wife as family caregiver—and pay his wife minimal maintenance or alimony. Allowing one parent to exit so casually runs contrary to the majority of marriage compacts, which are not intended as profit-making ventures but as commitments to live together and pool resources. I have an image of one of those famous circus families who form human pyramids. Imagine the mayhem if one of the brawny men at the bottom decided to leave the troupe while the members of his family were perched precariously overhead!

In giving the partner whose actions dissolved the marriage the right to initiate a divorce, these no-fault clauses violate a basic principle of our legal system: that wrongdoers should not be allowed to benefit from their misdeeds. Already fortified with money and malevolence, the wrongdoer gets a boost from no-fault in the form of a license to drive the legal machinery along with immunity from being condemned or penalized for crimes against his spouse and children.

Some states have dropped considerations of fault from both stages of divorce, the grounds for initiating the action and the guidelines for dividing property. This means that information on the wife's misery or the husband's venality is officially censored. One of the consequences is that judges more or less automatically order the sale of the home to produce cash for the couple to divide. This can happen even when the husband has absconded and pulled the plug on the family's entire life-support system.

Taking Nina as an example, we can compare what happened to her under no-fault with what modest protection would have been hers if her husband's violence had disqualified him from initiating the divorce.

Although Nina left home to protect her daughter from witnessing another assault, her husband could have misrepresented the facts and charged her with a fault ground, abandonment (but not aggressive abandonment); however, even the allegation of abandonment would not have held up in the face of the evidence of Howard's battering and provocation. Therefore, Nina could decide between stopping the divorce by disproving his claim of abandonment or turning the tables and charging him with cruelty so she would be the one activating the legal system. Either way, she would have been less of an underdog than in a no-fault proceeding in which Howard could sue and intimidate under no threat that he would have to answer for his violence.

It is the vague language of the three grounds for unilateral divorce—irretrievable breakdown, irreconcilable differences, and incompatibility—that makes it impossible to object or raise issues of fault. These allegations are self-fulfilling. Because the faithful wife can't refute the claim of "irreconcilable differences" when the abandoning husband has left home and will not attempt reconciliation, she can't even hold up the divorce until he has agreed to a fair financial settlement.

One wife protested, "It was infuriating that my husband could say *we* have irreconcilable differences and *we* have been living apart when the truth is *he* engineered the differences and *he* moved out of the house. I couldn't ask for a cooling-off period or for a chance to try therapy. I felt hoodwinked by the law."

The proponents of no-fault fret about people trapped in incompatible marriages by spouses who won't release them. The answer for this situation would be an honest one-party divorce, not misrepresented as no-fault and strictly limited to spouses who have met their social and financial obligations to the faithful spouse and children.

A growing number of lawyers and economists are sounding the alarm that women are losing economic ground under no-fault. Lenore Weitzman's major study of the economic impact of no-fault divorce, *The Divorce Revolution*, published in 1985, concludes:

> Divorce today spells financial disaster for too many women and the minor children in their custody. The data reveal a dramatic contrast in financial status of divorced men and divorced women of all ages and every level of marital duration. Women . . . experience a precipitous decline in standard of living within one year after divorce, while their husbands' standard of living improves. Older women and women divorced from men in the higher-income brackets ($40,000 or more) experience the most radical downward mobility.

Weitzman found that in the wake of California's conversion to no-fault, women were experiencing a 73 percent decline in their standard of living one year after the divorce while men were experiencing a 42 percent improvement, clear evidence that no-fault has been financially unfair to women!

Not everyone is willing to concede no-fault to be a culprit in the impoverishment of families. There is a tortured effort among lawyers and legal scholars to preserve no-fault in the financial settlement by fine-tuning the formulas. They would change the guidelines either by mandating a larger share to the homemaking spouse or by assigning more economic credit to the caregiver's contribution to the marriage. I'm afraid that the fine-tuners have never noticed the connection between dishonorable conduct during the marriage and nefarious maneuvers to conceal assets and deprive the innocent spouse of a fair financial settlement.

Many judges interpret no-fault guidelines to mean that breadwinners have to compensate the caregivers only for specific aid to their careers or for career opportunities lost in devoting themselves to caregiving, as if the social and emotional injuries of abandonment and divorce are reversible. So-called "rehabilitative maintenance," a brief period of what used to be called alimony, is awarded to tide a rejected wife over while she makes a transition to economic "independence." This is a cruel hoax. If the wife has dependent children, she has to commingle a job and single parenthood. If she is older, she is thrust unprepared and overage into the work force while her husband absconds to live handsomely on what would have been their retirement savings.

In a paper delivered in 1989 to the American Bar Association, Thomas M. Mulroy, a lawyer from Pittsburgh, cited a typical case of a mother's gradual decline to poverty. While the divorce proceedings were pending, "Sue" got alimony and child support in an amount of $2,150 a month, slightly less than half her husband's income, but the alimony stopped after the divorce. On her salary of $1,000 a month plus $850 child support from her husband, she couldn't keep up the payments on her house nor could she pay for services formerly performed by her husband such as baby-sitting, car repairs, and household maintenance.

> After [Sue] sold the house, she found that her qualifications for a new mortgage were limited. She moved into an inexpensive rental in a neighborhood where the schools were less good. When she had to have her gallbladder removed, she faced economic disaster. She had no disability benefits and poor medical coverage so she had to pay for herself . . . As she slid down the economic ladder, so did her children. Ultimately, she qualified for some public-assistance benefits to help get her by.

Valerie's experience of being abandoned by her husband and the legal system is typical of older women. When she was forty-five and her children were entering college, she went back to teaching and got an advanced degree that qualified her as a specialist in remedial education. Her part-time work satisfied her passion for helping children overcome learning problems but was not intended to supplement her husband's income, which was more than enough to support their life-style.

Ten years later, her husband bolted in the middle of the night but turned back in anger to fight her every step of the way during a grueling two-year divorce.

> "His assets vanished without a trace. My expensive, expert accountant told the judge that he must be hiding assets and income that would account for our lavish life-style, but the judge wasn't at all curious about the discrepancy."

191

"My husband and his lawyer argued that I could support myself with my teaching, and the judge agreed with them. I was awarded declining amounts of 'spousal maintenance' for three years only, leaving me on my own at the age of sixty. I did get the house, but it came with the mortgage my husband had taken out just before he left, so it had to be sold immediately."

As far as the judge was concerned, it was his job to help my husband dispose of me with as little inconvenience as possible. My infinitesimal pension was equated as an asset matching my husband's pension based on thirty-two years of employment and an income that was ten times mine."

Any theory that the nonworking spouse's entitlement depends solely on her contribution to marital assets leaves out what most of us value most about marriage: the social and emotional bonding. A wife's wholehearted participation in the marital relationship ought to legitimize her claim for support in a life-style comparable to her husband's whether or not she openly sacrificed a career to raise children or made a specific monetary contribution to either her husband's career or to the family's economy. The longevity of the marriage alone should suffice as evidence that the economic arrangement, whatever it was, had been acceptable to both partners.

Why shouldn't the humanistic contribution to a marriage count for as much as the economic contribution? The no-fault relegation of marriage to a business contract that can be broken at will with a judge dividing the exposed assets dishonors everything about marriage that has to do with integrity and commitment.

These all too typical settlements illustrate the inequity of attempting to distribute assets without considering fault and of comparing finances in the freeze frame when one spouse has sued for divorce. Without some longitudinal perspective, I don't see how there can be an outcome that is even moderately fair to the poorer spouse caught off guard by the divorce.

In fact, this characterization of the inherent unfairness of no-fault would apply also to the richer spouse if he or she were the one suddenly abandoned without cause. A number of lawyers reported that they are seeing a new trend of wives walking out and treating a long marriage as an investment to be liquidated on demand.

No-fault is neutral toward exploitation by either spouse of the other's decency.

The pattern seems consistent enough to be generalized. The poorer, weaker, more scrupulous, caregiving, innocent spouse has virtually no chance of obtaining a fair financial settlement so long as fault is ruled out of order in the proceedings.

No-fault legislation really sets a new priority for newlyweds: Protect your financial stake above all else; pursue your careers; leave your children to alternate caretakers; and don't risk your financial future by working at lower pay in one of the helping fields so you can spend more time at home with your children.

Susan Moller Okin has reviewed theories of justice as they have evolved in Western thought from Plato to now and discovered that one whole gender has been missing! There has never been an accounting for the role played by mothers in caring for and passing on social values to children. "To a large extent contemporary theories of justice, like those of the past, are about men with wives at home."

In the event of divorce, Okin holds that the economic contribution of the caregiver who raises the children and in other ways sustains the wage earner's day-to-day life should be valued as equal. Her novel solution is to equalize pay while the marriage is intact. She recommends that employers be required to make paychecks payable to both spouses, thus recognizing that "the household income is rightly shared, because in a real sense it is jointly earned."

11

No Fault, No Fairness

▼

Writing in a professional journal, Judge Warren Redman of Twin Falls, Idaho, challenged the theory that since it is impossible to decide which party is being truthful, both parties should be deemed responsible for the breakdown of a marriage:

"It is ludicrous to suggest that our legal system is sophisticated enough to assess and digest extremely complex factual and legal issues except when it comes to determining fault in divorce. . . .

"I suggest that we abandon no-fault divorce as inconsistent with the very nature of marriage."

Judge Redman points out that the only remedies available to compensate the injured partner—alimony, child support, and unequal property division—have been suppressed by the dictates of no-fault.

Even as applied to automobile accidents, the language of no-fault seems flawed. Innocent parties can be shortchanged, and drivers who cause accidents can easily deceive themselves about fault. It might be more accurate to refer to a no-fault settlement as "no *determination* of fault." This would dispose of the false implication that no one was at fault and replace it with the true implication that fault is simply too expensive to litigate.

With respect to divorce, no-fault instills a casual attitude that would never apply to automobile accidents. It's hard to imagine a driver interpreting no-fault automobile insurance as an invitation to reckless driving, but that's exactly what a husband who gets a sudden urge for abandonment reads into no-fault *divorce:* "The law says I can resign from our marriage anytime I please, and there will be no inquiry to determine which of us has damaged the other. Furthermore, the law will indulge me while I coerce you into accepting a puny *payoff*."

Preferring to believe in the good intentions of lawmakers, I have to assume that the men and women who drafted the models for no-fault thought that spouses would seek a divorce only after a long period of marital conflict and personal soul-searching. I also have to assume that, if given a choice, policymakers would put a higher value on protecting the faithful spouse and preserving the family than on greasing the wheels for the abandoning spouse.

The flaw in no-fault would become more evident if the deceptive language of mutuality were corrected. Labeling divorces in which there's been no wrongdoing on the part of the reluctant spouse "involuntary," "unilateral," or "one-party" would take away the implication of consent when the divorce has actually been coerced. It might also compel more accuracy in reporting about abandonment— a couple did not "separate" when one spouse deserted—and about divorces—a divorce should not be described as "bitter" or "ugly" when one spouse is the persecutor and the other is the victim.

Lenore Weitzman cites no-fault for contributing to the economic losses of women forced into involuntary divorce: "A major consequence of the no-consent (no-fault) standard has been a shift in power from the spouse who wants to remain married to the spouse who wants the divorce."

Writing in a publication of the American Bar Association, Harvey Golden, a matrimonial lawyer from Columbia, South Carolina, minced no words:

> The primary fault with no-fault is that it is an extreme, absolute position which ignores the fact that courts have rightfully and historically always been expected to make wrongdoers accountable for their transgression, whether in criminal, civil, or domestic courts, and anyone who thinks that there aren't any villains in domestic cases is an idiot, or a wimp, or is more interested in expediency than justice.

While the wife-rejection sequence is too subjective and psychological to be covered by legislation, the actions that comprise aggressive abandonment—withdrawing or walking out on a spouse without warning, provocation, attempting to conciliate, or preplanning for the family's social and economic survival—are specific enough to be argued and proved or disproved in a legal setting.

A judge would not need Solomonic wisdom to weigh evidence of financial and emotional abuse after separation. The following is a sampling of the abuse described by rejected wives: closing bank accounts; canceling home, health, automobile, and life insurance; stopping payments on mortgages; changing locks on doors and cars; physical assault; shredding clothes; neglecting children: attempting to push seventy-two-year-old wife out of moving car; removing wife's name from joint accounts; flaunting adultery in front of children; cutting off utilities; subterfuge to wipe out wife's savings; subterfuge to get information on wife's parents' estate; reneging on agreement to pay college tuition.

Having traced the course of wife rejection from the emotional pain to the economic losses, I feel that I would be betraying the trust of the women who shared these lacerating experiences if I didn't make a strong plea for some specific amendments to matrimonial laws to bolster the standing of the faithful spouse.

This proposal for categorizing aggressive abandonment as a marital fault, along with the traditional fault grounds of physical violence, cruelty, alcoholism, et cetera, is only the first suggestion in the box. I hope that victims, lawyers, and advocates for families will join in this discussion as well as the one on the mental-health aspects of wife rejection.

The benefits of classifying aggressive abandonment as a marital fault parallel those of naming the wife-rejection syndrome: People will recognize the crisis and the pattern of persecution.

A spouse contemplating leaving will know that it will be in his (or her) interest not to be charged with aggressive abandonment and that he will lose rights in the legal proceedings if he leaves without warning and preplanning for the family and will incur penalties if he engages in emotional and financial abuse after departure.

Divorce is never "normal," but everything is abnormal about divorces set in motion by the wife-rejection syndrome. These sudden departures or withdrawals are categorically different from separations or divorces that are rationally conceived. No discussion and no planning have preceded the breakup. The family's economic and social contract is operative one day, null and void the next. There has been no airing of differences, no attempt to repair the relationship, and no advance preparation for the welfare of the children. All communication based on reason and compromise stops, not to be resumed until and unless by accident, miracle, or act of therapy, the raging husband gives up his rage.

Part of the description of a rejecting husband is that he is laboring under a delusion of being persecuted by his wife. Without doubt, he will feel persecuted also by laws compelling him to safeguard her economic welfare, but remember, it was his choice to do nothing when he was experiencing waves of fear, panic, and resentment. He never let down his guard to talk about the turbulence that was endangering the marriage. It was his own undoing that he cloaked himself in deception, skidded into a bonding crisis, and ended up cannibalizing his family.

Here are some suggestions for procedures that would give more protection to rejected spouses and for penalties that might dissuade an abandoning husband/breadwinner (or wife/breadwinner) from engaging in economic warfare.

▶ Only spouses who could show that they have met basic obligations to their partners and children before and after separating would be permitted to file for a one-party divorce.

▶ Aggressive abandonment would make a parent ineligible for joint or sole custody unless the faithful spouse consents.

▶ An abandoned caregiver would have the right to go straight to court for protection, restitution, compensation, counsel fees, and penalties if the abandoning breadwinner engaged in financial coercion such as cutting off accustomed support, canceling insurance, turning off utilities, et cetera.

▶ Courts could fine abandoners for harassing their spouses personally, financially, or legally and could impose interest on arrears,

197

thus recognizing the unpaid debt for what it is—an involuntary loan from the dependent spouse.

The greatest favor to disadvantaged spouses would be an overhauling of the procedures to cut the costs of negotiating and litigating a divorce. Lawyers in small towns may charge "reasonable" fees of $75 an hour; in big cities the fees can run as high as $350 an hour (that's $5.83 a minute, one cent a second), and when two or more lawyers are working on your case, each of them may be charging a full or partial hourly rate while conferring together. The volume of paperwork—motions, cross motions, replies, answers, affidavits, subpoenas, briefs—is mind-boggling and only accessory to the main business of strategy, negotiations, and court appearances. Obviously, most women can't begin to pay for all-out representation.

Lawyers are not charitable institutions and are entitled to be paid for services rendered. Many work out long-term payments with their clients and give credit, anticipating payment from the settlement, but I have met women who told of attorneys who took liens on their homes and coerced them into signing promissory notes just before stepping into the courtroom.

Outside consultants are not likely to be called in to streamline procedures for divorce, but perhaps some legal scholars could be enlisted to examine these tangled, interminable proceedings to propose shortcuts that would reduce the costs without compromising the disadvantaged parties.

One alternative would be to apply the rules of evidence less rigorously to matrimonial proceedings—as is the practice in juvenile and family hearings. Lawyers are as hardheaded in matrimonials as they are in criminal trials, exerting themselves to the utmost to pounce on the opposition and block disclosure of information unfavorable to their clients. A forum that would permit the parties to tell a coherent, uninterrupted story would allow a truer picture to emerge than proceedings governed by the rules of evidence, allowing lawyers to harass witnesses with narrow questions designed to confuse, intimidate, or trap. (The rules of evidence could be more aptly described as rules for obfuscation.)

One worthy suggestion is for matrimonials to be heard in a separate tribunal presided over by trained hearing officers, a measure that would relieve overcrowded courts and increase the likelihood of fairer decisions for the parties.

Enforcing a settlement can be as expensive as arriving at it. It should not be necessary to appear with a lawyer to ask the court to compel a delinquent husband to pay his obligations. The courts are incredibly lenient toward men in default of financial orders, even wealthy men, rarely threatening them with the only effective deterrent, a jail sentence. A number of the women told of yielding to modest settlements for lack of money and stamina to fight on and then discovering when they returned to court to compel payment that the agreement was legally defective and therefore unenforceable.

It is really futile to try to squeeze a pleading for the rejected wife into the mold of no-fault. The rationale for protecting faithful spouses emerges from a radically different perspective on marriage and family, one that holds that marriage and family represent a healthy, reciprocal compact and that laws should be on the side of preserving the remainder of the family if that compact is broken.

Since the most expensive chunk of an adversarial divorce is locating the assets, it is the wives and children of self-employed husbands and fathers who are most easily cheated. Whereas salaries are hard to hide, it's not so difficult to alter records and transfer assets in your own business, be it a neighborhood dry-cleaning store or a megabucks venture-capital firm. Many people scoff at the possibility of hiding significant assets in view of the accountability demanded by the federal government. Obviously, law-abiding citizens inclined to be fair to their families are not acquainted with the methods of cheating that seem to come naturally to a sector of divorcing husbands.

To do justice to the rejected or abandoned spouse, one-sided fault has to be a major influence on the settlement. Unless the law tells judges to protect the injured party, the demands of the vindictive spouse who has money and the will to fight will inevitably prevail either by defeating justice or costing the innocent party so much money that the effect is the same.

Marjory's former husband is a case in point of the vendetta that never ceases. Of all the wives, she was the one whose love and trust of her husband most seemed to match mine. When she was compelled to make an economic settlement, she asked only for the house (which came with a mortgage) and for the property she and Daniel had bought together as an investment for the children. "Even the judge thought I was entitled to more, but my pride wouldn't let me wrangle with Daniel."

Daniel, unfortunately, was not looking for resolution. Having moved cross-country with his girlfriend, he returned twice within ten years to bring lawsuits to attempt to wrest the real estate investment for himself. He lost both times, but it cost Marjory over $120,000 just to protect for her children the minimal settlement the court had already awarded her.

Mary Ann Glendon calls for a "children first" principle, closer to the practice in most Western European countries. "The judge's main task would be to piece together from property and income and in-kind personal care the best possible package to meet the needs of the children and their physical custodian."

When I visited Felicia and her children in their modest half house and silently compared it to the very comfortable, well-groomed surroundings they lived in when she and Oliver were married, I was flooded with feelings of injustice.

Why shouldn't the settlement enable the children to live as well with their mother as they would have lived with their father if he hadn't abandoned them? Oliver, whose income was derived from earnings and inheritance, was enjoying his accustomed life-style, but his children's had declined in every respect. Their mother's income had been reduced by about two-thirds, while her responsibilities had increased exponentially.

Felicia is now a single parent responsible for two small children. She receives income and child support from her settlement but must supplement it with a full-time job to meet current expenses and save for the future. Now she must handle all of the administrative problems connected with managing a family. She has to pay professionals for a multitude of services that used to cost nothing, such as the financial management that was contributed by her husband and the chores that were shared in the less pressured atmosphere of a two-parent household. Her new home is in a neighborhood where she has no support system—no husband, neighbor, or relative—to back her up when somebody is sick or something goes wrong.

To add to these burdens, she is still harnessed to Oliver's volatility. Six years later, he is somewhat subdued, even remorseful— his vendetta spent—but "incapable of spending time with the children without causing monumental emotional upsets. By the time I put out the fires from the last visit with their father, it is time for another. He indulges and disappoints, winds them up for frantic activity and scolds when they become overwrought.

"Both children are in therapy, for which he pays, but they need constant compensation from me to manage the tension that stems from his mercurial behavior. His emotional needs are so consuming that he can't register or respond to theirs."

Felicia, nevertheless, counts herself lucky "because the settlement would have been much worse if it hadn't been for my lawyer friend who represented me without charging and my woman friend who propped me up to demand more than the pittance Oliver tried to foist on me."

(After the divorce, Oliver's success quotient went up. This reflects the disconcerting fact that "bad-object rage" does work for some wife rejecters. After deserting and vilifying their wives, some of the husbands seemed to regain their capacity for productive work. As income climbs—too late for the divorce settlement, of course—hostility recedes. Having steeled themselves to expect malevolence, the wives are astonished to encounter their former husbands and find them benign, even overtly friendly.)

Lenore Weitzman's study of post-divorce incomes after no-fault was adopted in California is the most comprehensive. Her in-depth interviews give a truer picture than can be gleaned from court papers.

Research in other states has confirmed the trend first noted in California. A 1988 study by James B. McLindon comparing settlements in New Haven, Connecticut, before and after no-fault found wives much less well off, echoing Weitzman's findings as well as studies in Colorado and Vermont. All the researchers concluded

201

that wives lose and husbands gain. One reason is that the husband retains his income-producing capacity so that his "equal" share consists of assets that generate income while the value of the wife's share, often the house and a modest supplement for child support and transitional maintenance, is fixed.

To plead the case for the faithful partner is not possible without raising emotional issues that tough-minded people are supposed to suppress in the age of no-fault. Prevailing opinion doesn't endorse entering a marriage as if it were a business decision but has no patience with the spouse who resists terminating a marriage as if something more than a business partnership were at stake.

There was a very telling scene in *Another Woman*, Woody Allen's serious film about relationships. The jilted wife walks in accidentally on her ex-husband's prenuptial party, and everybody is stupefied.

My first reaction was exactly like that of the guests—I wanted the party spoiler to leave; she was embarrassing me. But ex-wife was feisty enough to ask wife-to-be to identify herself. "Which one of you is Marion?"

I found the unladylike shrill in her voice more embarrassing when she charged her husband with betrayal. "You were at the Holiday Inn while I was in the hospital having my ovaries removed."

It was only when she elbowed her husband as he was propelling her to the door that I suddenly began to identify with her humiliation and impotence. I watched that scene three more times for the vicarious satisfaction of those brief stabs of defiance. Thank you, Woody Allen, for giving your audience a momentary glance at what it's like to be the victim instead of the indulger in infidelity.

By the end of the film, Marion had learned some lessons about adultery. Why, she wondered, should she be surprised that her husband, so guilt-free about betraying Wife Number One, would instigate an affair that would betray Wife Number Two?

Not only do we live in a climate of opinion in which injured parties are irritants, there is little compassion for dependency. Wives should know better than to become financially dependent on their husbands. It is the fate of children to be dependent on their parents' largess—or lack of it—and therefore to lose the privileges of affluence when their career-centered father divorces their home-centered mother.

An attitude that marriage should be subject to cancellation with the same ease as membership in the Book-of-the-Month Club would inevitably breed impersonal rules for dividing the income and property on which the parties to that marriage depend.

There are fair and honorable ways to end a marriage, but there is nothing fair, honorable, *or* mutual about one spouse routing the other and nothing unfair about weighing fault, insisting on accountability, and seeking judicial authority to protect the innocent members of a family.

The above principles embolden me to plead for a division of the property and possessions of a long marriage in favor of the single parent left in charge of the family. It would serve justice to insist that the husband who abandons aggressively for a new life without his wife and children deposit a sufficient share of his past and future earnings to continue the family's standard of living. Thus, the faithful spouse would be entitled to most of the material possessions that were accumulated during the marriage, *plus* enough assets and income to maintain the preabandonment life-style.

Unfortunately, this principle would be of little help to lower-income families who live on the father's salary. There is no pot to divide, and angry fathers are not good prospects for child support unless their wages can be attached. The only source of supplement for the lower-income family is the public sector. Mary Ann Glendon advocates modeling ourselves on our Western European counterparts, who provide more as-of-right services and income supplements for children to reduce the poverty of single-parent families.

How much better it would be for children and parents if services like day care, dental and medical insurance, after-school programs, and higher education were provided as-of-right so middle-income mothers would have more discretionary money and lower-income mothers would have a cushion without having to subject themselves to the humiliation of qualifying for welfare and being hounded to demonstrate their neediness.

There is also a role for government in preserving marriages. Programs to prevent and relieve the stress of unemployment and health crises might make it possible for more men to stay at home and cope instead of running away to escape anxiety. More could be done to help families deal with bereavement, alcoholism, and drug abuse, the triggers for so many divorces.

Sylvia Ann Hewlett cites the United States as singular among advanced industrialized nations for having the highest divorce rate and the poorest provisions for families. Our divorce rate is from two to twenty times higher than that of other Western nations, yet our support system is "shamefully weak and shrinking, a loss of 21% in the four years between 1981 and 1986." Hardest hit are custodial mothers, the majority of whom have to carry all the physical and financial responsibilities for rearing children.

Applying family-first standards, the faithful spouse would get the family home whether or not there were offsetting assets. There seems to be a pattern among rejecting husbands, sometimes abetted by state laws, of pressuring for the home and, failing that, of forcing its sale as a stipulation of the financial settlement. (Felicia's experience is typical. "Our house was sold before I realized it was on the market.") It is a measure of the flight into self-justification that a rejecting husband would never concede that his hasty departure in any way compromised his rights to the real estate.

In putting her home ahead of other financial interests, Kathy was typical of the wives in the study. Because Alex left in ecstatic pursuit of a second round of fatherhood, she had no time to collect her thoughts or emotions before bargaining the terms of the divorce. To keep the house, she had to surrender her stock in the business to which she had made a significant contribution.

> We had just reached the point where we could take some of the profit for ourselves instead of reinvesting in the business. Alex got the asset that generated income and provided an expense account and tax benefits. I got the asset burdened with a mortgage and deferred maintenance. I could have sold the house to realize capital, but that would have meant moving to smaller quarters in a less desirable neighborhood and further depleting our daughter's sense of security.

I don't mind working to support myself, and fortunately, I have some marketable skills. What I hate is having no one with whom to share problems and responsibilities. Both my daughter and my mother had health problems last year, and I couldn't afford the air fare or the time away from my job to be with them. Families need someone free to be the caregiver. I think their medical care suffered and I know that my absence was an emotional blow to them as it was to me.

Even under pressure, Kathy had the wits to insist on more than her husband's verbal promise to pay their daughter's tuition. She accepted reduced maintenance for herself in exchange for incorporating a clause on tuition in the settlement. "We had always planned to give our children as much education as they wanted. I didn't expect Alex to fight this, but wanted to play safe since I couldn't earn enough money for tuition. That I would have to spend three years in court to collect was beyond my imagination."

Priority for making the family whole would give rejected wives claims on the major components of survival: the family home, and a source of income to keep the family solvent. A presumption in favor of the innocent wife's uncontested right to the family home would signal wives and children that justice is on the side of maintaining the family.

Recent changes in federal guidelines that will raise the minimum amounts of child support are only a midget step in the right direction. Mothers are supposed to be miracle workers after divorce—earning promotions in well-paid jobs and managing their children in their spare time. Felicia estimates that she works a full 110 hours a week! It's probably unfortunate that some women succeed at this Herculean labor because matrimonial laws seem to be based on these exceptional women, implying that normal, conscientious mothers are inferior for feeling overwhelmed by their responsibilities.

Children of abandonment really deserve full-time mothers to help them cope with the stresses. Whether the children retreat into sadness or express their hurt with defiance, they invariably make enormous emotional demands on mothers already preoccupied with economic survival.

Listening to a lecturer on couples therapy boldly propose that divorce now be accepted and integrated as a full-fledged stage in the life cycle, I interrupted to inquire what he had in mind for the children: "Everything we know about children tells us that constancy is what they need most in their development; divorce leaves them feeling permanently betrayed." There was an embarrassed silence in the room; an older woman, a psychiatrist, did stop afterward to lend support to my unpopular position.

Now we have evidence from Judith Wallerstein's follow-up of sixty families fifteen years after the divorce to document what everyone knew but was afraid to admit: that many children never recover from the shock of their parents' divorce.

Divorce has created a new underclass of college students, those who have been made poor by matrimonial laws that allow noncustodial parents to stop supporting their children on their eighteenth birthday. How infuriating to be deserted by a father whose higher education included advanced degrees from prestigious universities and how humiliating to have to plead for the tuition that would have been paid automatically if your father hadn't left home! Mothers report that the colleges penalize the student for the father's repudiation by basing entitlement to financial aid on parents' combined income even though the father categorically refuses to support his child.

If family-first propositions seem utopian, it may be a reflection of the numbing effect of the no-fault environment, which is so indifferent to the welfare of dependent members of the family compact. A husband discards his wife as if she were nothing more than refuse from his past, and the law—instead of addressing how she should be compensated—asks how quickly she can be recycled into any low-paid job so her husband will be free of lingering debts.

As mentioned before, no-fault principles result in judicial orders to sell what for most couples is their major asset, the family house, to produce cash for the financial settlement. This obligation to convert assets to cash for a settlement comes ahead of humanitarianism. Sometimes, mothers are allowed to live in the home until the children reach college age, but there is no mercy for the hardship caused by this enforced sale or for uprooting an older wife whose husband abandons her in a late-life bonding crisis.

Three principles would have to be incorporated in the guidelines for dividing property to yield even modest fairness to disadvantaged spouses, in whose number I would include spouses with any mix of the following: less income, less property, less will to fight, less experience in adversarial confrontations, less desire for a divorce, and less record of engaging in unscrupulous tactics.

The first principle would be to bring fault back as a major influence on the settlement. Guidelines based on no-fault cast judges as impartial referees, whereas their legislative mandate should be to protect the legal and financial rights of the disadvantaged party.

The second principle would be a presumption that the spouse who had been cruel and malicious either as a marital partner or a divorcing adversary should be scrutinized carefully for dishonesty in the financial disclosure.

The third would be a presumption that spouses who are intimidating and abusive toward their partners in the divorce are not to be trusted to keep their commitments to their former families.

So far as I know, no one has singled out for study divorces in which there was a pattern of one-party persecution; consequently, there are no statistics on settlements to support an intuition that the unmonied, innocent spouse can't possibly emerge with a fair share of the assets. If research were published demonstrating the high correlation between one-sided fault and impoverishing settlements, those members of the bar and the state legislatures who concern themselves with family issues might have ammunition to demand corrective amendments to the laws governing the division of property.

Even in states where fault appears in the guidelines for settlements, the judges often refuse to hear about abuse or injuries unless the allegations are very serious—attempted murder, for instance. To learn what standards are applied in any particular state or county, it's best to consult members of the matrimonial bar.

In addition to giving fault priority in the guidelines for dividing property, here are other suggestions for amendments that might serve to improve the economic prospects of abandoned wives and children.

207

▶ Compel abandoning monied partners to pay, at the commencement of the case, counsel fees sufficient to cover the extraordinary cost of obtaining financial information normally withheld by partners who hold title to the assets.

▶ Mandate courts to redistribute assets and award alimony to produce an ongoing stream of income to support the abandoned wife and children.

▶ Instruct judges to compensate the faithful spouse for being left to shoulder family responsibilities alone.

▶ Give judges discretion to estimate the shortfall between the assets disclosed and the income that was obviously available to support the couple's life-style and to increase the award to the dependent spouse accordingly.

▶ Mandate the courts to protect children's financial interests so mothers are not burdened or conflicted having to bargain simultaneously for themselves and their children.

▶ Enact federal regulations to compel states to raise the age of parental responsibility to include the years of higher education.

▶ Devise provisions to ensure that the breadwinner will keep his agreement to pay college tuition, such as some form of savings or trust fund to guarantee that money will be there when the child reaches college age.

▶ Institute more aggressive measures to enforce payment of child support including a presumption that those fathers who balk at paying support while the divorce is pending are the ones to be closely supervised for compliance after the divorce is final.

▶ Index alimony and child support to increase in tandem with income, expenses, and cost of living so inflation won't pauperize families dependent on alimony and support.

▶ Award the family home and its contents, other than personal belongings, to the faithful spouse, earmarked for inheritance by the children of that marriage, when there's been serious fault or aggressive abandonment.

The item on possessions appears at the personal request of wives who watched their sentimental possessions being carted off to another household. They felt that after a long marriage there should be an understanding that the marital holdings stay with the faithful spouse and descend to the children and grandchildren.

Enforcement of rules discouraging aggressive abandonment would, of course, have to be gender-free. Wives would also be penalized for ending marriages with abruptness, cruelty, and callous disregard for the survival of their husbands and children. A dependent spouse who commits aggressive abandonment would not be entitled to the even split that would have been her share if she had ended the marriage with decent regard for the future welfare of her husband and family.

To quell the doubts of those who feel that women are almost always the victims, let me say again that the spouse who leaves home to escape abuse should not be confused with the spouse whose departure is a curtain raiser to annihilating attacks on his mate. Both testify to the need to protect the innocent members of a family from being exploited as scapegoats.

To answer the doubts of those who predict more acrimony from extended debates over fault, let me say that disputes over finances—whereabouts of assets, what constitutes joint and separate property, and who deserves credit for what economic contribution to the marriage—are just as rancorous as disputes over personal injuries with the difference that in the former, the innocent caregiver is the one on the defensive. The caregiver must rely on her lawyer's cleverness in demonstrating her contribution to the marriage as a business partnership. It helps if her lawyer can show that she supported her husband while he obtained a graduate degree or furthered his career by managing the household or subordinated her professional opportunity to advance his.

The only subject that is ruled out of order in so-called no-fault divorces is the pain and suffering one partner has caused the other, and the only contributions that don't win points are humanistic ones like ethics, self-sacrifice, integrity, fidelity, nurture, devotion.

No-fault neutrality meshes conveniently with an undercurrent of opinion that views marital misery as self-inflicted. If judges and lawyers choose to believe that a beleaguered wife deserves what she gets for having married such a scoundrel in the first place, then they can justify not exerting themselves to help her.

The missing information, of course, is that lovers are deceptive, and they are not inclined to disclose their unconscious defenses on the application for a marriage license. Once the wooing is over, the previously adored spouse may be slotted for blame instead of praise, and if the time ever comes, even in middle or old age, that a scapegoat is needed, it may come to pass that the formerly adored spouse is the one to be sacrificed.

If the legal system doesn't want to recognize a vendetta. If it refuses to distinguish between false and true accusations. If it takes the hands-off view of "a plague on both your houses" or "where there's smoke, there's fire" or of "splitting the differences"—regardless of how one-sided the abuse and deprivation—then the legal system is every bit as implicated in vandalizing the lives of innocent women and children as the incurably enraged wife rejecters.

All the folklore to the contrary, it definitely doesn't take two to tango.

12

Latest Entries

▼

Four years have passed since the early morning phone call that irrevocably ended twenty-five years of marriage and family life.

My mental health has improved slightly in that I no longer sink into a depression between six and eight in the evening nor does my stomach feel as if it were being churned by a garbage disposal each time I have to face a group of strangers. Still, if there is such a thing as soul-ache, that is the name I would give to the sadness that envelops me from the moment I regain consciousness in the morning until I drift off to sleep late into the night.

The most encouraging thing I can report is that my children are somewhat less estranged. Almost as if their moves were being choreographed, they began coming through the door with arms outstretched, instead of elbows stiffened to stave off an embrace.

It is so gratifying to be a parent again that I am obliging their censorship regarding Arthur, my husband, their father. I am forbidden to mention our past or to ask questions about his present. It seems like a small price to pay for the tropical warmth that fills me inside when I am with my children, but I know I will have to settle for a strained, superficial relationship so long as it is taboo to discuss the subject that has torn us apart.

It is common for children to scold their rejected mothers: "Dad doesn't complain all the time the way you do." They also reproach her for being a poor sport if she is confrontational enough to remind them that Dad is neither lonely—having provisioned himself with a new girlfriend before leaving—nor poor—having absconded with the income and savings that were intended to support their old age.

As for Arthur, it looks as if he will live out his days in silence and denial, his memory of me deleted, his mind clamped shut so his conscience will never know how he has blighted forever the lives of the people who loved him best. It torments me that I will never know the truth of my marriage. Was it imagination or reality that I lived with and loved a man whose passions and sentimentality were so finely attuned to mine?

The company I keep now is almost entirely women and almost entirely women I have met since Arthur left. Not surprisingly, many of them are in one stage or another of postabandonment trauma—some, like myself, having been deserted by husbands who seemed loving and reliable, more by husbands who seemed enamored of their wives but less than honorable in business and personal practices, and still others by husbands who aborted their marriages rather than answer for infidelity or dishonesty.

As a group, we are gifted at comforting one another, but also fragile, like people suffering from the same disease.

Just as you can't fix your friend's cancer, you can't intervene with the legal system to get her some justice. We are too well behaved to break into court decorum and plead with the judge to divert some of the income and savings our friend's husband is expending on a mistress so that his wife of forty-two years will have some money and possibly feel less suicidal.

Besides their heartache and bruised self-esteem, abandoned wives are notable for managing with a geriatric infrastructure: clothes that were fashionable ten years ago, cars with motors that are on life-support systems, refrigerators so noisy that the whole house reverberates, peeling paint, leaky faucets. No microwave ovens or VCRs; telephone-answering machines are the single technical extravagance to be found in these homes.

As I become educated about financial settlements, I realize that the jeopardy lies not only in the minuscule amounts that are awarded but in how easy it is to lose a good part of a lump payment in a bad investment. A trusted adviser—whether carelessly or conscientiously—steers a divorced wife to a "safe" investment (nothing speculative) which promptly declines in value, shrinking her already undersized nest egg.

Yes, women would be well advised to take precautionary measures and educate themselves on plumbing and finances, but not anticipating abandonment, the duplication of labor seemed unnecessary.

Each time our informal coffee-cum-comfort group gathers, there are new members grateful for the chance to share and explore and get advice from veterans. To my amazement one Sunday, the group around the table is co-ed. Two men have joined us, and they both report experiences that fit the rejection syndrome. How extraordinary to spend two years tracking every lead to a man who might describe a breakup that followed the pattern of the syndrome and then meet two rejected husbands in one afternoon!

The same sickening pattern. A wife who is cherished by her husband starts behaving "strangely"—detached, critical, unenthusiastic about joint activities. The husband diagnoses the change as a reaction to a stress event, like a death in the family, and outdoes himself being understanding and undemanding.

One man said his wife had pleaded for "space" to allow her to work through her conflicts. Trying to accommodate, he moved in temporarily with members of his family. Only when he attempted to return home did he discover that he had been accommodating an affair. His wife promptly moved out, leaving him to assume full care of their severely disabled son. He had to change jobs immediately to be near the child's school. To compound the emotional despair and financial emergency, she pulled up a van while he was at work and stripped the house bare. Unable to afford a lawyer of his own, he left the divorce arrangements entirely to her lawyer and never claimed the child support to which he would have been entitled.

Within a week, I met two more husbands aggressively abandoned by their wives and attacked in the blistering way that goes with the rejection syndrome: departure without warning; no second thoughts or compromise; insults and demands that feel like intentional persecution; adultery calculated to humiliate; false accusations that can be decoded as projections—blaming another for one's own misdeeds; financial chicanery; and coldhearted cruelty.

For what it is worth as a reflection of gender differences, the men were consistent in depicting themselves as "walking around like a zombie," a slight variation on the "I was a basket case" flashback of the wives. I asked the men whether they objected to the syndrome being called *wife* rejection since women outnumber them as victims. No objections.

At the same time I was eliciting information on wife rejection from victims, I was also seeking illustrations in literature. Novelists and playwrights would surely understand love-hate reversals, but no examples surfaced, leading me to suspect that it would be difficult for writers to make such sudden, total renunciation believable to readers or audiences.

Then in the winter of 1990, *The War of the Roses* was released and the gap was filled. This film, with its screenplay by Warren Adler, who wrote the book of the same title, could pass for a documentary on the rejection syndrome.

Many critics pegged *The War of the Roses* as a dark comedy, its novelty a marital conflict exaggerated beyond credibility. The reviewer for the *Los Angeles Times* took it more seriously, observing that the drama of love turned to hate seemed to strike a raw nerve with the audience.

For me, the unbearable moment was seeing the daggers-in-the-eye fury in Kathleen Turner's expression when, as Barbara Rose, she informs Oliver (played by Michael Douglas) that their eighteen-year marriage is over. "I don't want to be married to you anymore."

Barbara Rose's incipient hostility intensifies into bad-object rage when she is summoned to the hospital where her husband has been taken with a suspected heart attack. Writhing in pain and fearful that he will die before his wife arrives, Oliver scribbles a love letter. The crisis, which had the effect of reaffirming Oliver's passion, has the opposite impact on Barbara: It crystallizes her detestation. By no means relieved when it turns out to be only an intestinal disorder, Barbara spews out her rejection. She would have been "happy to be free [of him] . . . like a weight being lifted."

One of the women in our group recalled waking up desperately ill with what turned out to be pneumonia and reading the unmistakable message on her husband's face that he would leave her to die if she couldn't get help herself.

Barbara's terminal fury at her husband really starts as an internal squall. Feelings of disgust and contempt seem to gather and then—like the rejecting husbands whose wives I interviewed—she erupts in rage and attempts to eject him as if he were overloading her lifeboat. Whether he deserves this treatment is irrelevant. Typical of rejecting spouses, she has deleted all positive memories of her marriage. One would never guess that this husband has been faithful and attentive and has earned the substantial income that supports their upper bracket life-style and their shared passion for a well-endowed home.

Like most suddenly rejected spouses, Oliver reacts with stunned disbelief. You can't be serious. . . . I still love you. I still want you. . . . You'll get over this. He also disregards his wife's assaults and her dire warning: "You have no idea what I'm capable of."

Oliver seems to take it as a macho challenge to thwart Barbara's outrageous demand that he disappear and hand over the house and all its contents to her. Obviously, he has no premonition of the Chernobyl effect—the allergy she has acquired to her husband and all of his attributes. Oliver, in fact, is so confident that he can rekindle the sexual flame that he blocks out the stinging words of rebuke and physical revulsion: "When I watch you eat, when I watch you take a step, when I look at you, I want to smash your face in."

Not long after that, Barbara leaps onto a chandelier to get away from her husband, he jumps on to save her, and they both drop to their deaths.

Other than misrepresenting the gender of the majority of rejecting spouses (husbands do most of the abandoning), the film faithfully reproduces the syndrome and its repercussions. What was unusual about Barbara Rose was not that she discharged so much venom on her husband as she came under the influence of bad-object rage but that she attached herself to the house instead of a lover to compensate for coming unbonded from her husband. Oliver Rose was exceptional in his obstinacy. He wouldn't retreat even when his wife made it abundantly clear that she was deranged enough to kill him.

Of course, it would be hypocritical for me to criticize anyone else for being obtuse or persevering. I certainly persisted after a therapist, hinting at the Chernobyl effect, told me that my husband would be "ruthless" in keeping me away. Unless it is spelled out for you, it's hard to grasp that your husband, whom you still love, will necessarily injure you because he will act on delusions that you are carrying toxins that will poison him.

One lesson of the *Roses* is that no wife or husbnd, not even one as confident, successful, rich, and handsome as Oliver Rose is a match for rejection and rage. One inference is that if the genders had been reversed and the rejecting spouse had been the husband-moneymaker, he would have emptied the family treasury, leaving his wife so indigent that she couldn't have paid the mortgage or the medical bills or put food on the table.

The conclusion seems inescapable that the time is overdue to label the wife (or spouse) rejection syndrome and to move on to changing private attitudes and public policy toward abandoned spouses and the children who depend on them. Ostracism and impartiality, the current favored responses to abandoned spouses, are a far cry from the kind of disaster relief that could be available if government, professionals, and friends formed a common front to mobilize money and comfort for the survivors.

Glossary

Wife-rejection syndrome—for the chain reaction that starts with a trauma provoking such intense anger, guilt, and shame that a spouse defends unconsciously by displacing and projecting a lifetime of stockpiled grievances onto his or her mate.

Bonding crisis—for the state of anxiety and the remediating delusion that one's spouse is the cause of the distress and that relief consists of breaking away and forging a new intimacy. Panic, crying, false euphoria, adultery, "bad object rage," and the "Chernobyl effect" are among the visible signs of this intimacy crisis.

Bad-object rage—for a fierce and prolonged fury toward another person, e.g., a spouse, who has been unconsciously diagnosed as the bad part of the self that must be rooted out and punished to escape self-destructive anger.

Chernobyl effect—for the aversion and distancing from an intimate, e.g., a spouse, whose physical presence sets off feelings of panic and dread as if she or he were "radioactive" or a hazard to survival.

Aggressive abandonment—to give legal definition to the pattern of financial deprivation, coercion, false charges, and emotional persecution that typifies the aggressive conduct of rejecting spouses *after* abandonment. As opponents, they are brutal and punishing at every stage of the divorce. Even after the settlement is concluded, they continue to wage legal warfare either directly by bringing lawsuits that have no merit or indirectly by refusing to pay debts and forcing the former spouse to file lawsuits to compel payment.

NOTE: If *malice* were substituted for *abandonment*, the term **aggressive malice** could be applied more broadly to categorize and punish the behavior in divorce of a belligerent spouse going to extremes to hurt and deprive a former partner who has never been injurious or vengeful.

Bibliography

Sources referred to in the text and those that are relevant for further reading on negative projections in relationships, emotional misunderstandings, and couples therapy.

Arendell, Terry. *Mothers and Divorce*. Berkeley: University of California Press, 1986.

Balint, Michael. *The Basic Fault*. New York: Brunner/Mazel, 1968.

Boszormenyi-Nagy, Ivan, and David N. Ulrich. *Foundations of Contextual Therapy*. New York: Brunner/Mazel, 1987.

Bowen, Murray. *Family Therapy in Clinical Practice*. New York: Jason Aronson, 1978.

Cain, Barbara S. *"Parental Divorce During the College Years."* *Psychiatry*. Vol. 52, May 1989, pp. 135–146.

Chesler, Phyllis. *Mothers on Trial: The Battle for Children and Custody*. Seattle: Seal Press, 1987.

Chodorow, Nancy. *Reproduction of Mothering: Psychoanalysis and the Sociology of Gender*. Berkeley: University of California Press, 1978.

Dicks, Henry. *Marital Tensions: Clinical Studies Toward a Psychological Theory of Interaction*. New York: Basic Books, 1967.

Fairbairn, W. R. D. *An Object Relations Theory of Personality*. New York: Basic Books, 1954.

Gaylin, Willard. *Feelings, Our Vital Signs*. New York: Harper & Row, 1979.

———. *The Killing of Bonnie Garland*. New York: Simon and Schuster, 1982.

Gillis, Phyllis. *Days Like This*. New York: McGraw Hill, 1986.

Glendon, Mary Ann. *Abortion and Divorce in Western Law*. Cambridge, Mass.: Harvard University Press, 1987.

Golden, Harvey L., and Michael J. Taylor. "Fault Enforces Accountability." *Family Advocate*, Winter 1988.

Goldstein, Joseph, Anna Freud, and Albert J. Solnit. *Beyond the Best Interests of the Child*. New York: Free Press, 1973.

Goleman, Daniel. *Vital Lies, Simple Truths: The Psychology of Self-Deception*. New York: Simon and Schuster, 1985.

Golton, Margaret. *Your Brain at Work: A New View of Personality and Behavior*. New York: Frank Publications, 1983.

Gordon, Thomas. *Parent Effectiveness Training (P.E.T.)*. New York: New American Library, 1975.

Halperin, James, and Ilse Halperin. *Projections: Our World of Imaginary Relationships*. New York: Seaview Putnam, 1983.

Hendrix, Harville. *Getting the Love You Want*. New York: Henry Holt, 1988.

Hewlett, Sylvia Ann. *A Lesser Life: The Myth of Women's Liberation in America*. New York: Warner Books, 1986.

Horney, Karen. *The Neurotic Personality of Our Time*. New York: W. W. Norton, 1937.

Johnston, Janet R., and Linda E. G. Campbell. *Impasses of Divorce: The Dynamics and Resolution of Family Conflict*. New York: Free Press, 1989.

Kernberg, Otto. "Factors in the Psychoanalytic Treatment of Narcissistic Personalities." *Journal of the American Psychoanalytic Association*, Vol. 181, pp. 51–85.

Kerr, Michael E., and Murray Bowen. *Family Evaluation*. New York: W. W. Norton, 1988.

Klein, Melanie. *Envy and Gratitude*. New York: Delacorte, 1975.

Kohut, Heinz. "Thoughts on Narcissism and Narcissistic Rage." *The Search for the Self*, Vol. II., edited by Paul Ornstein. Madison, Conn.: International Universities Press, 1978.

McLindon, James B. "Separate but Unequal: The Economic Disaster of Divorce for Women and Children." *Family Law Quarterly*, Spring 1987.

Miller, Alice. *Drama of the Gifted Child*. New York: Basic Books, 1981.

Mulroy, Thomas M. "The Faults of No-Fault: Effects of No-Fault on Child Support." Annual Meeting Compendium, American Bar Association, 1989.

Okin, Susan Moller. *Justice, Gender, and the Family*. New York: Basic Books, 1989.

Pennebacker, James W. *Opening Up: The Healing Power of Confiding in Others*. New York: William Morrow, 1990.

Person, Ethel Spector. *Dreams of Love and Fateful Encounters*. New York: W. W. Norton, 1988.

Pittman, Frank. "The Masculine Mystique." *The Family Therapy Networker* (Special Feature: "Men Nurturing Men"), Vol. 14, No. 3, May/June 1990.

———. *Private Lies: Infidelity and the Betrayal of Intimacy*. New York: W. W. Norton, 1989.

Redman, Warren. "Coming Down Hard on No-Fault." *Family Advocate*, Winter 1988.

Rheinstein, Max. *Marriage Stability, Divorce and the Law*. Chicago: University of Chicago Press, 1972.

Rogers, Carl R. *On Becoming a Person*. Boston: Houghton Mifflin, 1961.

Rubin, Lillian. *Intimate Strangers*. New York: Harper & Row, 1983.

Rubin, Theodore I. *The Angry Book*. New York: Macmillan Publishing Company, 1969.

Scarf, Maggie. *Intimate Partners*. New York: Ballantine Books, 1987.

Scharff, David C., and Jill S. Scharff. *Object Relations Family Therapy*. New York: Jason Aronson, 1987.

Shapiro, Stephen A. *Manhood*. New York: G. P. Putnam's Sons, 1984.

Solomon, Marion F. *Narcissism and Intimacy: Love and Marriage in an Age of Confusion*. New York: W. W. Norton, 1989.

Strean, Herbert S. *Extramarital Affairs*. New York: Free Press, 1980.

————. *Resolving Marital Conflicts: A Psychodynamic Perspective*. New York: John Wiley & Sons, 1985.

Tannen, Deborah. *You Just Don't Understand: Men and Women in Conversation*. New York: William Morrow, 1990.

Wallerstein, Judith S., and Sandra Blakeslee. *Second Chances—Men, Women and Children a Decade After Divorce: Who Wins, Who Loses—and Why*. New York: Ticknor and Fields, 1989.

Weitzman, Lenore J. *The Divorce Revolution: The Unexpected Social and Economic Consequences for Women and Children in America*. New York: Free Press, 1985.

Wile, Daniel B. *After the Honeymoon*. New York: John Wiley & Sons, 1988.

————. *Couples Therapy: A Non-Traditional Approach*. New York: Wiley-Interscience, John Wiley & Sons, 1981.

Willi, Jurg. *Dynamics of Couples Therapy*. New York: Jason Aronson, 1984.

Winnicott, Donald W. *Collected Papers*. New York, Basic Books, 1965.

————. *The Maturational Processes and the Facilitating Environment*. New York: Basic Books, 1965.

Index